GROWING
ORCHIDS
UNDER LIGHTS

D1329404

Charles Marden Fitch
Photographs by author

Series Editor James B. Watson

2002 *Revised Edition*

American Orchid Society
Delray Beach, Florida

GUIDE

American Orchid Society

Contents

Front Cover (left to right): Agrosun lamp, *Rhynchocentrum* Lilac Blossom, *Cattleya* (Jungle Spots x *amethystoglossa*) (inset), light garden (inset), *Paphiopedilum* Mem. Gerald Lawless 'Haley Suzanne', HCC/AOS (bottom). *Back Cover (top to bottom): Miltonia* Lover's Point 'Lion Star', HCC/AOS, *Phalaenopsis* (Fortune Buddha x Sara Lee) 'Talisman Cove', *Dendrobium* Thai Gem. *Opposite:* (left) *Angraecum* Compactolena 'Talisman Cove', (right) *Phalaenopsis* (Sambambo x *lueddemanniana*).

Growing Orchids Under Lights © 2002 American Orchid Society, 16700 AOS Lane, Delray Beach, Florida 33446-4351 (telephone 561-404-2000; fax 561-404-2100; e-mail TheAOS@aos.org; Web site orchidweb.org). Library of Congress Catalog Card Number 2001 132033. ISBN 0-923096-03-5. Text and photographs © Charles Marden Fitch. Portions of this book were previously published in two other books by Charles Marden Fitch: *The Complete Book of Houseplants Under Lights* (Hawthorn Books, Inc., New York, 1975) and *All About Orchids* (Doubleday & Company, Inc., Garden City, 1981). The opinions and recommendations that may appear in this publication regarding the selection and use of specific plantcare products, including but not limited to pesticides, fungicides and herbicides, are those of the individual author, and not those of the American Orchid Society, which neither adopts nor endorses such opinions and recommendations and disclaims all responsibility for them. When selecting and using such products, readers should seek and obtain the advice of the manufacturer and of responsible government agencies. 01.6.7M

Introduction

ORCHIDS WILL GROW ALMOST anywhere under broad-spectrum fluorescent lamps. Using fluorescent lights to supplement natural daylight is a practical way to keep orchids healthy in dim windows and shady sections of a greenhouse. Some lamps, such as the reflector spots and floods, are useful for displays and theatrical highlighting of blooming plants, especially at shows. Powerful high-intensity lamps can change a spare room into an orchid-growing range. *Growing Orchids Under Lights* explores the many ways that artificial electric lighting can help you grow and display orchids.

I concentrate on practical fixtures that can be purchased at hardware stores or by mail order. Household fluorescent fixtures and standard lighting fixtures for tungsten lamps have many applications for orchid growers. Details and some first-hand recommendations from orchid growers who use high-intensity specialized fixtures are included.

Growing Orchids Under Lights offers practical suggestions for using lights in several ways in the home and greenhouse. These include supplemental fluorescents, tungsten lamps for display effects, fluorescent fixtures for indoor light gardens and high-intensity lamps. Chapters on the cultural requirements of orchids grown under lights explain how to meet the plants' needs in this special environment, and there is an encyclopedia of hybrids and species recommended for growing under lights.

Fluorescent lamps have always been part of my orchid-growing techniques. I use them to supplement daylight in my greenhouses, for mirrored displays in a living room and as the major source of grow light for orchids in the basement. In researching it, I have discovered how other orchid growers use lights to help their orchids thrive. This book is designed to help you utilize lights for growing and display.

Growing Orchids Under Lights

Opposite: A compact cattleya hybrid set in a saucer of moist gravel shares the spotlight with companion tropicals. A fixture like this, with two 20-watt lamps, is enough for display lighting so orchids in flower can be enjoyed in the home. *Above:* These paphiopedilums, shown here in a sunroom, were grown and brought into flower under fluorescent lights in a basement.

1 ~ The Quality of Light

CONTROLLED EXPERIMENTS AND practical findings in home light gardens confirm that the quality of light — the band of colors called the spectrum — is as important to plants as the intensity or quantity of light. Once, growers believed that brightness alone was the primary factor in determining whether their orchids would prosper and bloom. Now it is understood that green plants need certain colors of light to initiate normal cycles in growth and blooming.

The blue and red rays in the visible spectrum are essential for photosynthesis. Through this complicated process, plants with chlorophyll (the green coloring matter) capture light energy and transform it into an organic form of stored energy for growth. For this process to occur with optimum efficiency, plants require adequate and balanced light.

Of the near-visible spectrum, far-red light is also important for sturdy growth. Subtle variations in wavelength and combinations of various colors (blue with red, for example) interact to enhance photosynthesis. Laboratory research has discovered in green plants a light-sensitive pigment called phytochrome. This pigment is cued or activated by slight changes in red and far-red light.

One wavelength of red light programs the phytochrome to encourage maturation, ripenings, and dormancy, while a slightly different part of the red spectrum (far-red and invisible infrared) signals cell activity, thus stimulating plant growth and new foliage.

Artificial lights, to induce optimum development, must contain the required spectrum. Sunlight contains all the necessary light rays plus other portions of the spectrum not so important to plants. The green and yellow portions of light, although most important in human vision, are not so important to green plants. It is mainly the blue rays that promote foliage growth and the red rays that foster flowering.

Lamp Choices

Manufacturers of fluorescent tubes have employed these findings and those of their own independent research to develop lamps formulated to enhance plant growth. By combining various rare powdered chemicals (phosphors), they can customize the spectrum of a fluorescent lamp and thereby create a color balance of maximum value to plants.

The horticultural lamps are higher in output of blue and red rays than are common household lamps, such as Cool White. The Gro-Lux lamps, for example, have about three times more usable red energy than Cool White lamps.

The type of fluorescent tube used is less important when the artificial light is only to supplement sunlight. At a window, in a greenhouse or bright sunroom where plants get the major portion of light from the sun (and thus receive the full spectrum), fluorescent supplemental lighting can be effective in standard Cool White/Warm White or related deluxe types that are slightly warmer in color.

If you wish to match supplemental light with daylight, choose one of the lamps balanced for noon daylight color, such as Vita-Lite or Verilux TruBloom. They increase brightness and extend light-hours without altering the natural color of midday sun.

Lumens

Manufacturer's specifications indicate the actual brightness of fluorescent tubes in lumens. Light output from fluorescents drops fastest during the first 100 hours of use, so companies traditionally publish figures showing effective brightness after 100 hours.

A sample of 40-watt tubes shows the

General Electric Cool White Lamp with a light output of 3,200 lumens, the Verilux with 2,168 lumens and a Sylvania Daylight tube with 2,600 lumens. Sylvania lists no lumens for Gro-Lux lamps.

The lumen figure shows only what a lamp is giving off in brightness. How much of the light actually reaches the plants depends on reflector size and color, distance between lamps, and between lamps and foliage. Light measured at the plant position, the actual light received by the foliage, is measured in footcandles. These measurements show only brightness. Fluorescent lamp color (the spectrum) is also an important factor in the efficiency of a tube as shown by tests mentioned earlier.

The brightness at any distance from a light source is traditionally given in footcandles, a measurement of visible light easily made with a foot-candle meter or converted from readings on a sophisticated photographic light meter. The more foot-candles shown, the brighter the light. Foot-candle measurement is important in estimating adequate illumination for work

areas, and in creating proper contrast ratios in photography or television recording.

Since brightness is only one of several important factors in growing houseplants under lights, foot-candle measurements are of little value. Watts per square foot, observation and tube type are more practical considerations. Nevertheless, since light intensity is important, you may notice variations in plant response under different fluorescent lamps. Some of the difference will be due to brightness. For example, the brightness range between three popular fluorescent lamps shows that Cool White tubes have more visible light, which can be measured in foot-candles, and thus the Cool White tubes look brighter. The standard Gro-Lux tube, which has a rosy glow, is only 34 percent as bright, and the Wide-Spectrum Gro-Lux is 72 percent as bright as Cool White.

Where brightness is a significant factor, as for high-light-requirement orchids (*Ascocenda, Cattleya, Dendrobium, Vanda*), choose from the dimmer Wide-Spectrum Gro-Lux, similar broad-spectrum lamps for their improved light spectrums or high-intensity-discharge lamps (which are discussed in detail in Chapter 7).

To obtain maximum brightness, put plants slightly closer to the horticultural lamps, or set the tubes closer together, thus providing more watts per square foot. A 2- to 4-inch space between lamps is efficient.

Practical Approach

The multitude of factors that influence healthy growth include heat, light color, light intensity, day-length, night-length, temperature and air circulation. The following points present a more practical system of measuring suitable light intensity for your plants.

After more than 30 years of growing hundreds of species and hybrids under lights, I know that you will have success if you follow these guidelines:

■ Arrange lamps 4 to 12 inches above foliage in fixtures with at least two tubes and a bright-white or aluminum reflector. A 40-watt tube is more efficient than two 20-watts.

■ Use horticultural fluorescents or combinations of broad-spectrum horticultural lamps with Cool White lamps for best results with a wide variety of flowering plants.

■ Set an automatic timer to give 14 to 16 hours of light per 24 hours, reduced to 12 hours for eight weeks in early winter.

■ Provide environmental conditions required by the species you wish to grow — usually relative humidity of 40 to 60 percent and a temperature in the 60s at night, into high 70s during light hours.

Slight yellowing of foliage or excessively compact growth indicates that light intensity is too strong. The solution is to increase distance between plants and tubes.

Above: A light-intensity meter will measure foot-candles of sunlight, high-intensity-discharge lamps and fluorescent lamps.

Sparse blooming on normally floriferous species, very deep-green foliage or leggy, drawn-out growth show that light intensity is too low. The solution is to move lamps closer to the plants, perhaps increasing the number of lamps if you are using only one or two tubes.

Lamp Condition

New lamps are brighter than those that have burned 75 to 100 hours. Therefore, new lamps can be placed somewhat farther above foliage than older lamps. For example, if your orchids have prospered for a year with lamps 10 inches above foliage and you replace the lamps all at once, move the fixture 4 to 6 inches higher for the first 75 to 100 hours of use.

Another system is to keep lamp-to-foliage distance constant but replace tubes one at a time over a period of weeks. This works for fixtures with two to six tubes and guards against sudden yellowing of leaves.

BANDS IN NANOMETERS	WARM WHITE		COOL WHITE		STANDARD GRO-LUX		GRO-LUX/WS	
	WATTS	PERCENT	WATTS	PERCENT	WATTS	PERCENT	WATTS	PERCENT
Ultra-Violet < 380	0.13	1.52	0.16	1.68	0.10	1.42	0.27	3.16
Violet 380–430	0.46	5.15	0.72	7.57	0.70	9.67	1.07	12.48
Blue 430–490	1.15	12.91	1.98	20.78	1.96	27.07	1.22	14.29
Green 490–560	1.80	20.24	2.35	24.67	1.02	14.02	1.24	14.49
Yellow 560–590	2.06	23.17	1.74	18.27	0.10	1.42	0.83	9.77
Orange 590–630	2.13	23.95	1.69	17.75	0.44	6.05	1.36	15.93
Red 630–700	1.03	11.53	0.81	8.47	2.86	39.55	1.86	21.78
Far-Red 700–780	0.13	1.53	0.07	0.81	0.06	0.80	0.69	8.10
TOTAL	8.89	100.00	9.52	100.00	7.24	100.00	8.54	100.00

Above: A comparison of energy emission in arbitrary color bands of 40-watt fluorescent lamps, in watts and percent of total emission.

2 ~ Supplementing Sunlight

USING ARTIFICIAL LIGHT TO supplement sunlight is practical in home window growing areas, in greenhouses and for flasks of seedlings or tissue-cultured plantlets. In addition to encouraging sturdy growth, light is an important element in creating dramatic displays, as shown in Chapter 4.

Window Growing Areas

Orchids thrive in front of windows when the intensity and duration of sunlight suit the genera. When sunlight is insufficient, there are several options: Add fluorescent lamps above the windows and even along the sides of the panes. Simple valances can hide the lamps from view. Consider making the valances a decorative element by creating them from especially attractive wood such as driftwood or split bamboo. A valance that is painted or covered with a suitable fabric is another possibility. Increase light reaching the plants by paint-ing nearby surfaces white or by using mirrors to reflect light. A white ceiling above the windows will also increase the efficiency of each lamp.

The easy way to control lighting is with simple wall switches. When it is desirable to have the lights on every day for a specific time, then an automatic timer would be more practical. Contract a licensed electrician to install the timer if it needs to be wired into existing electrical wiring. This will eliminate cords from multiple fixtures strung around.

To have the light blend with natural daylight, use lamps with 5,000 Kelvin temperature. These lamps provide light that is the same color as sunlight at noon, which guarantees the flower colors will be true. Chapter 4 has more details about lamp colors.

Highlights

Install tungsten fixtures overhead to feature specific orchids in a window display. Lamps with built-in reflectors provide directional control within limited space. Reflector floods cover a wider area than reflector spots. Choose the type best suited to the growing space.

Tungsten lamps give off much more heat than fluorescents. If your hand feels very warm when held at the same level as the plants under tungsten lamps, the fixtures are too close. If the distance between orchids and the lamps cannot be increased, install weaker bulbs.

A general rule for using fluorescent

Left: High-intensity-discharge lamps burn 5 am to 9 pm in a New York greenhouse where phalaenopsis are raised. Supplementing natural light with artificial light can transform almost any area into an environment in which orchids will grow and flower.
Opposite: A wealth of orchids can be grown under lights. Phalaenopsis are especially popular, including this *Phalaenopsis* Fantastic Stripe 'Talisman Cove' (Mae Hitch x Kathleen Ai).

lamps — as total source of light or to supplement daylight — is to use the largest lamp possible. For example, if you have an 8-foot window choose an 80-watt fixture rather than two fixtures of 30 or 40 watts. Larger fixtures provide more light per electric dollar than two or more fixtures, thereby saving money on electric bills. This recommendation applies to all areas in which fluorescent lamps are used, especially if they are on many hours to provide the primary source of light for growing.

Greenhouse Lights

One way to fully utilize all areas of a heated greenhouse is to light dim sections with supplementary fluorescent lamps.

In my lean-to greenhouses, the bench sections close to the supporting house wall get less afternoon sun than the outside section. To keep orchids growing well, I have fixtures of two 40-watt lamps, each hung against the house wall. Under the benches I use fixtures with four 40-watt lamps because these sections receive almost no direct sunlight. Supple-

mental fluorescent light is an excellent way to maximize the humid heated greenhouse space.

It is important that all fixtures in a greenhouse be grounded. With water being splashed around, the electrical grounding is a required safety precaution. Consult with an electrician to gain advice on how to develop a light setup in the greenhouse that is safe and meets local code restrictions.

It is also an advantage to have fluorescent lamps above each bench to light plants for night viewing and to brighten cloudy days. Use narrow fixtures with reflectors just slightly wider than the lamps, to allow sunlight to reach the orchids. Under benches, where little light comes from above, I use standard wide reflectors that are an integral part of aluminum fixtures made for horticultural applications. In a large greenhouse with enough headroom, high-intensity-discharge lamps, hung above the plants, can supplement daylight. In dim winter months, high-intensity-discharge lamps can be timed to come on two hours be-

fore sunrise, or extend the "day" after sunset.

Flasks and Compots

Fluorescent lamps are a cool safe light source for flasks of seedlings, tissue-cultured plantlets and recently transplanted community pots. Orchids in flasks can be quickly damaged if the bottles are overheated by sun. Keeping bottles in shady areas or indoors away from the direct sun becomes practical when you provide fluorescent light.

When orchids are first transferred from flasks into community pots they are vulnerable to sunburn and quick drying. Fluorescent lighting is the safest way to provide a constant source of light for sturdy growth. In modern orchid-propagation laboratories, fluorescent lights are a standard for illuminating racks of flasks.

Growers in tropical countries where outdoor temperatures and light intensity may be too much for flasks keep bottles in air-conditioned rooms with fluorescent lamps providing the major source of growth light.

Opposite: Metal-halide lamps with safety-glass shields supplement sunlight in a rainforest greenhouse. The lamps burn 6 am to 12 pm.
Top: A lean-to greenhouse turns a living room into a light-filled sunroom where orchids grow. Night display is lighted by overhead flood lights.
Above: Rothara Koolau Starbright 'Elizabeth' grows 10 to 12 inches tall and will flower twice a year when well grown.

3 ~ Light Garden Design

YOU CAN DESIGN INDOOR LIGHT gardens to be a decorative highlight in any room or to be a utilitarian growing range with emphasis on maximum utilization of space. Ideas for both approaches are presented here. In my collection, I have some pure growing areas with no special care to a pleasant presentation because blooming plants are brought to other places for display.

In the living room, it is a different matter. When orchids depend on fluorescent light for growth yet are always on view, it is worthwhile to create a light garden that is both functional and aesthetically pleasing. Some commercially produced light-garden fixtures are attractive enough to be kept in a living area. If certain features of a pre-made fixture are unacceptable in your setting, consider modifications.

You can paint fixtures and frames to suit your decorating plans. An entire fixture or light-garden cart could be framed by attractive molding, hidden by sliding panels, kept behind sheer curtains or incorporated into an outdoor-style arbor of bamboo, rough wood or rattan. A basic precaution is to retain adequate access for daily care of your orchids.

Layout

When growing areas are totally illuminated by artificial light, arrange benches close together directly under the lamps. With plants on benches or racks right below the fixtures they will receive maximum light intensity. Peripheral areas around and below the benches are good places for foliage plants and seedlings that require less light than mature, flowering-size plants.

Above: A collection of orchids under broad-spectrum fluorescent tubes in a New York City apartment bloom well because the eight 40-watt lamps cast intense light.

Growing Orchids Under Lights

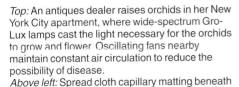

Top: An antiques dealer raises orchids in her New York City apartment, where wide-spectrum Gro-Lux lamps cast the light necessary for the orchids to grow and flower. Oscillating fans nearby maintain constant air circulation to reduce the possibility of disease.

Above left: Spread cloth capillary matting beneath plant containers to provide humidity and a source of moisture for roots. The soft material is easily cut to fit trays.

Above: A drain hole with a removable plug is one feature of the fiberglass Flora Cart tray, which measures 20 inches wide, 29 inches long and 1½ inches deep.

Growing Orchids Under Lights

4 ~ Displays

WITH THE SKILLFUL USE OF artificial light, it is possible to create a display of blooming orchids anywhere in the home, office or at an orchid show. In a home setting, fashion permanent display areas where the fluorescent illumination matches daylight. With lamps of 5,000 Kelvin, the light blends perfectly with natural light coming from windows. For additional control, directional tungsten reflector spots or floods are useful but these lamps give a warmer look that flatters pinks and reds, but is too distorting for blue flowers.

Double the Beauty

Double the flower show by backing the display area with mirrors. In the home or show setting, mirrors are the perfect way to give an expanded look to tight quarters. Mirrors also let one appreciate the backs and side views of front-facing flowers. This an important advantage with complex flowers like orchids.

Inexpensive mirror panels are easy to glue on any flat surface. When your budget permits a more elaborate arrangement, consider installing top-quality wall mirrors. Use the largest possible size for each situation to maximize the flower display and light reflection.

Combined Lighting Effects

A display area for orchids in bloom is especially appropriate when a major portion of the collection is raised totally under lights in a spare room, detached building or basement. Create a display area in living quarters using mixed lighting effects. For example, broad-spectrum

Above: A sunroom with standard Gro Lux fluorescent lamps looks attractive even at night. The daytime light is natural sun. Fluorescent lights are placed beneath the benches.

Opposite: A mirror used in a light garden will double the floral beauty while increasing brightness, here from Verilux Instant Sun fluorescent lamps.

Growing Orchids Under Lights

fluorescent lamps, hidden from direct frontal view by ornamental covers of wood, plastic or metal, can be arranged to provide overall illumination.

The general light level need not be high because it is designed to sustain orchids in bloom, not to provide strong light for new growth. Even though the level may be rather low, it will soon become obvious that orchids with moderate light-intensity requirements will often make healthy new growths. Phalaenopsis and paphiopedilums are two genera that can do well when set several feet away from fluorescent lamps, especially if the plants get a few hours of natural light each day.

Add screw-in tungsten floodlights in wall or ceiling fixtures. These tungsten lamps, available with built-in reflectors (PAR lamps), are useful to highlight special plants. An arching spray of oncidiums or cymbidiums looks dramatic at night when illuminated by a tungsten flood or spotlight. Keep such lamps far enough away from the orchids. Feel the leaves under the lamp. If foliage is warm, then increase the distance to protect the plant.

Get hints for display-area design by attending regional orchid shows. Some attractive features for a display area include:
■ Small fountains with recirculating water.
■ Companion foliage plants such as anthuriums, bromeliads, dwarf palms and begonias.
■ Driftwood "trees" on which orchids can be hung.
■ Beautiful or interesting rocks.
■ Moss and Spanish moss (*Tillandsia usneoides*) to soften spaces between features in your display area, or to hide supports.
■ Small fan to keep air moving and gently move foliage of companion plants.

Changing Scene

A major joy in having a special display area is rearranging the composition as new orchids come into bloom. Every few weeks, take away plants past their prime. Bring in orchids with open flowers. Once orchid flowers are ripe, the plants can be moved without danger to flower presentation. Remember that de-

Growing Orchids Under Lights

Opposite: Reflective Mylar on a wall in an orchid light garden increases beauty by reflecting color and shape. Like mirrors, Mylar also increases brightness.
Top: Light quality influences the success of an orchid display. Orchids grow well and flower colors look natural under Verilux Instant Sun 40-watt fluorescent lamps.
Above: The high-intensity-discharge Agro Sun high-pressure-sodium lamp has a good light spectrum for growing orchids, but flower colors do not appear natural.

veloping buds are photo-sensitive (light seeking). If you reposition a plant just as buds are maturing, the flowers may twist toward the brightest light. Sometimes this results in an unattractive floral orientation, but it is not harmful to the plant.

Rotate companion plants in your orchid display garden. Grow foliage plants under ideal conditions, with bright light, so they will be compact. Flowering companions such as begonias, African violets and anthuriums raised for flowers all thrive under four 40-watt broad spectrum lamps. Once they have flowers you can move them to lower light intensity in your display area for a month or more of sustained show. Foliage companions such as ferns, palms and philodendrons will thrive for years in medium-level light, under orchids, or around the edge of light gardens.

Top: A combination of sunlight and overhead fluorescent lamps brighten a display area with a northern exposure. A dendrobium (right) and paphiopedilums (center) are among the orchids on view.
Above right: Phalaenopsis thrive under three 40- watt lamps mounted on the wall with mirrors behind. A waterproof tray keeps floor below dry. *Opposite:* A phalaenopsis joins African violets in a small light garden illuminated with a circline fluorescent lamp. The light is adequate for keeping the orchid healthy while it is on display.

5 ~ Lamps and Fixtures

IN THE HOME, AS SUPPLEMENTAL light for a small greenhouse or sunroom, and as the main light source for indoor growing ranges, fluorescent lamps are the most practical. The bright high-intensity-discharge lamps are discussed in Chapter 7, although they are not as easy to use or live with as common fluorescents.

Fluorescent lamps will fit in anywhere orchids are to be grown. In temperatures of 50 to 90 F, fluorescent lamps deliver safe bright light with minimum risk of burn, noise, glare or explosion. The electrical requirements are also reasonable, especially with modern high-efficiency ballasts.

High-intensity-discharge lamps are useful in rooms or a greenhouse where you will not spend much time, but are not recommended for places where you will linger. The color of high-intensity-discharge lamps, even "daylight" types,

is more artificial than fluorescent lamps such as Instant Sun or even Wide-Spectrum Gro-Lux. Orchid flowers look different under different light sources. The flowers are most attractive under fluorescent lamps that match noon daylight color temperature, technically listed at 5,000 degrees Kelvin to about 6,000 degrees Kelvin.

Orchids will flower best when given a wide-spectrum-type light. Seedlings grow well under plain cool white or common household daylight lamps, but adult orchids often fail to bloom well if given only limited-spectrum light. Fill fixtures with Wide-Spectrum Gro-Lux lamps for the lowest-cost broad-spectrum light source. If you also wish to have the truest color for viewing flowers, select one of the lamps that offer both a broad-spectrum and daylight-type look.

Reflectors

Use reflector fixtures over basement plant tables, under greenhouse benches, and in other places where four to six inches can be spared for a reflector. Baked white enamel and polished aluminum reflectors are both suitable. Aluminum reflectors are lightweight and bright, but after a year or so they need scrubbing with a cleanser to get rid of the dulling film that forms. If you paint aluminum reflectors with flat white metal paint, you need to wipe them occasionally.

Baked-enamel reflectors are standard with most fixtures; the white surface is excellent but the metal construction is heavy. Some popular plant stands and tiered carts, such as the Flora Cart (Tube Craft Co.), come with white steel reflectors. Fixtures from several companies feature all-aluminum construction.

Table Stands

The simplest way to provide light

over plants is to buy fixtures constructed for light gardening. They are usually supplied with convenient switches, efficient reflectors, and some provision for hanging. Legs to permit fixtures to stand free are available from some manufacturers.

Opposite: Fluorescent bipin lamps have a small crease in the metal rim. Line this up with the socket opening for the longest life of rapid-start lamps. *Above:* A sturdy metal Flora Cart turns a cellar or spare room into a bright growing area. The fixtures hold four 40-watt lamps that cast adequate light for many orchids.

Table Fixtures

When you don't want to hang or permanently install a fixture, purchase one of the self-supporting units designed to stand on legs above a plant tray. Typical of this design is Sylvania's Gro-Lamp and the portable Combolite of Tube Craft. Waterproof trays of plastic, fiberglass or aluminum to fit neatly under these light fixtures are offered by various suppliers.

Some companies offer tabletop kits complete with waterproof tray and free-standing fluorescent fixture suitable for placement on a table or other flat surface. If you cannot find the color tray or fixture that complements your decor, simply cover the exterior of reflector and tray with paint. But keep the inside of a reflector white and do not paint the polished aluminum part.

Circline Fixtures

The round table lamps designed for plants are fitted with circline tubes. Most of these are supplied with efficient Wide-Spectrum Gro-Lux lamps, which are excellent for orchids and companion plants, such as African violets and similar tropicals. The one drawback to the circline units currently offered is that the push-in light switches will not work automatically on timers. It is necessary to turn the units on manually, but a timer can turn them off.

However, desktop circline fixtures are practical and attractive. They are well suited to offices, since lovely flowering and foliage plants can be kept growing with little space or care required. Fill the tray with moist gravel (adding water pe-

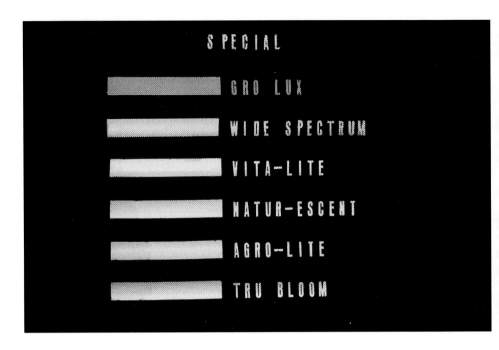

S PECIAL

GRO LUX

WIDE SPECTRUM

VITA-LITE

NATUR-ESCENT

AGRO-LITE

TRU BLOOM

riodically to keep it moist) to provide humidity. Leave the light on from morning to late afternoon, but not for 24 hours a day.

Above: Each type of fluorescent tube emits a specific color. Here, a comparison of a few of the many fluorescent lamps available for orchid light gardens.

Tiered Stands

Professionally built stands with two or more levels for plants often make the most efficient light gardens, especially where you wish to grow many plants in a limited space.

To customize a commercial light stand, paint the frame and fixture tops with your choice of color. Rust-Oleum and similar metal paints work well on reflector tops. Aerosol cans make even painting easy, but spraying should be done outside or in a well-ventilated room away from plants. Brush application is best where it is necessary to paint near furniture. Permit all parts to dry several days before placing plants on the stand.

For efficient operation, fixtures usually have an accessory plug input so two or more units can be plugged together. The terminal light fixture is then plugged into the timer connected to an electric outlet. All fixtures then go on and off si-

multaneously, according to how the timer dial is programmed.

Several stand designs are offered in catalogs. For example, Hausermann Orchids markets the Orchid Garden — a 74-inch-tall, two-tier light stand created to meet the needs of orchids. The fixtures hold four 40-watt (48-inch) lamps each over a 22x48-inch adjustable tray. An optional third tier tray and light fixture combination will increase the growing area and overall height.

Indoor Garden Cabinets

Several glass cabinets designed for growing orchids incorporate light fixtures. Often these are elaborate and expensive sophisticated growth chambers supplied with controls for heat, humidity, ventilation, and light. Some manufacturers offer the cabinets in several finishes, making it possible to choose one that complements the decor of your interior.

Orchids Under Different Types of Lights

A metal halide 400-watt lamp has a color temperature of 4,000 Kelvin and an overall yellowish tint that gives an unnatural color to flowers and foliage.

The Verilux Instant Sun fluorescent lamps use a blend of four phosphors to produce natural-looking white light of 6,280 Kelvin.

Wide-spectrum Gro Lux fluorescent lamps offer a blend of light color that encourages sturdy plant growth. Plants look attractive under this light.

Standard Gro Lux fluorescent lamps have a rosy hue that makes red and pink tones glow, but makes blues look odd. Plants grow well under these lamps.

6 ~ Equipment and Timers

THE FIXTURES SOLD FOR LIGHT gardening are usually designed to fit into a metal rack, sometimes with several levels adjustable by changing chains. Other fixtures are wall-mounted. In a situation where the light fixtures need not look attractive, you can save money by hanging basic reflector fixtures from overhead beams on chains.

In a basement, spare room or garage light garden where emphasis is on maximum efficiency, consider arranging hanging fluorescent fixtures over portable benches. Each fixture, hung from overhead supports such as bolts in the ceiling or wood beams, can be adjusted by simply inserting metal hooks into the chain. Fluorescent fixtures sold in light-garden catalogs come with efficient reflectors, on-off switches and holes for chain hooks at each end.

Safe Approach

All fixtures used for light gardening must have grounded plugs to prevent harmful shocks. Even with careful watering, it is inevitable that water will occasionally splash onto fixtures or drip onto plugs. Grounded fixtures help keep the light gardener safe. Fluorescent lamps burn so coolly that water will not cause the lamps to explode. This is not true of tungsten lamps and high-intensity-discharge bulbs. With these hot-burning lamps, arrange all fixtures well above any area that will be wet or that might be hit when you are watering.

Timers

Select timers according to the total power they must control.

Inexpensive timers sold in hardware stores for home use usually can handle at least 800 watts, more than enough for the average home light-garden cart with three fixtures of four 40-watt lamps each. Read the label on the timer to determine how many watts the unit can handle. Simple timers turn the fixture on when you want, and turn them off after a specified duration. More-sophisticated timers offer several light period durations. For orchid growing, it is sufficient to use simple timers that turn fixtures on at the start of your light-garden day, then shut them off when darkness is desired.

Larger Light Gardens

For extensive light gardens, those using many fixtures or using several high-intensity-discharge lamps, it may be beneficial to invest in a dedicated electric line with a powerful commercial timer. Those designed for commercial greenhouses can be installed to control a bank of wall plugs. All fixtures plugged into this specific line will be controlled by the master wall-mounted timer. Be sure

that this is installed by a licensed electrician and that all outlets are grounded.

Protection

Arrange fixtures so air can circulate. Ballasts give off heat that needs to escape into surrounding air. This heat is useful during cool weather because it reduces the amount of artificial heating needed to warm the growing area. Orchids also do best when their light hours are warmer than nights. For safety, place fixtures under water-deflecting material if you plan to do overhead watering, as in a greenhouse situation. Protect fixtures under benches by placing a fiberglass or cement compound (Eternit, etc.) panel just under the bench bottom, with a slight tilt toward one end. This waterproof material will channel any water away from fixtures below. A fire extinguisher for electrical fires is good insurance in light gardens. Keep one at the entrance of each growing area and know how to use it. Check with your local fire department and hardware store personnel to find an extinguisher that is suitable and affordable.

Opposite: The Plant Life aluminum fluorescent fixture holds four 40-watt lamps and has a high-efficiency ballast to save electricity.
Top: The Super Grow Wing fixture, with a 400-watt high-intensity-discharge lamp, comes with a UV glass filter (right) and remote ballast (left).
Above: Fixtures exist for every need, including this stand that holds flasks of orchids raised from seed and from tissue-cultured meristem clumps.

Growing Orchids Under Lights

Selecting the Right Equipment:

These fluorescent fixtures are internally grounded through a three wire plug.
A <u>potential</u> <u>shock</u> <u>hazard</u> exists if the mating plug is not grounded in like manner.
If a three wire system is not available, it is recommended that the fixture be externally grounded, with a piece of wire, to a suitable ground connection, such as a water pipe. GROWER'S SUPPLY CO., MICHIGAN

Above: A grounded electric wire plug is important for fixtures used in wet horticultural settings such as indoor light gardens and when placing fixtures beneath greenhouse benches.

Above: A precision hygrometer is useful to measure relative humidity in your plant-growing area. Most orchids thrive with 50 to 60 percent relative humidity.

Four Elements to Consider

Above: An automatic timer for plant lights that mounts on a flat surface has a grounded s-wire plug and metal lid to keep water away from the inside.

Above: A screw-base fluorescent reflector bulb fits into a standard socket, but uses less power than tungsten lamps. This is a 15-watt Osram reflector lamp.

7 ~ High-Intensity Lamps

HIGH-INTENSITY-DISCHARGE lamps, often listed as HID, are useful for growing orchids because the fixture ballast and lamp combinations produce bright light efficiently. Orchid growers who use HID fixtures typically devote an entire area to light gardening, well away from living spaces. The ultra-bright light and odd color rendition make HID lamps better suited as light sources in spare rooms, basements and greenhouses. For supplemental light in living areas it is more practical to use fluorescent lamps in commonly available 40-watt fixtures. However, fixtures and bulbs are available today that are attractively combined into handsome units that fit into a home's decor.

Lamp and Fixture Types

There are two types of HID lights available for the home gardener: metal halide and high-pressure sodium. Metal-halide lamps have light that is high in the blue spectrum, promoting foliage growth. Coated-metal-halide lamps have a slightly higher red spectrum.

High-pressure-sodium lamps produce light higher in the red-orange color spectrum, promoting flowering. HID lights range in wattage from 50 to 1,000 watts. The wattage of the bulb (lamp) affects the square footage of growing area it effectively covers. The 250-watt lamp covers approximately a 3x3-foot primary growing area (maximum intensity), and a 4x4-foot secondary area. The 400-watt system covers a 4x4-foot primary area and a 6x6-foot secondary area. A 1,000-watt lamp will cover a 6x6-foot primary area and an 8x8-foot secondary area. What this means is that the most intense light is in the primary area. Less intense

400 watt
DAYLIGHT

Above: Orchids show natural color when photographed with a daylight-balanced flash (Diamond Box Balcar reflector). Compare this with their color when under HID lamps.

Above: A 400-watt daylight-balanced high-intensity metal-halide lamp gives balanced spectrum with more normal color than standard HID lamps.

but beneficial light is provided in the secondary (outlying) area.

HID lighting fixtures are made specifically for a single metal-halide or high-pressure-sodium lamp and must be the same wattage as the fixture used. Each fixture has its own ballast and the lamp used must be the same type (base up or horizontal) as the fixture design. Only universal lamps can be burned in either base up or horizontal position. High-pressure-sodium lamps provide higher lumens (light output) than metal-halide lamps. The sodium lamps also have a longer effective life. Because of their higher wattage, the HID fixtures and lamps run hotter than incandescent or fluorescent lights. Plants are generally kept farther from HID lamps, and for some plants or rooms, should be combined with a ventilation system. The 430-watt Son Agro lamp is balanced for plant growth and a more pleasant color, having 30 percent more blue-band light. Study current suppliers' catalogs for the most modern designs in fixtures and the best lamp type for your application.

Above: High-intensity-discharge (HID) lamps are useful for indoor horticulture, including the growing of orchids. This 400-watt Agrosun lamp emits a light spectrum that is balanced for plants.

A Success Story

Many members of the American Orchid Society have had success growing a wide range of genera under HID lamps. Some of their techniques have been well documented in feature articles in *Orchids — The Magazine of the American Orchid Society*. Here is how Robert Weltz Jr, prize-winning orchid grower, explains his success with high-intensity lamps:

Many years ago good friends of mine received as a present 50 cattleyas for their greenhouse. Knowing my love for plants and of my green thumb, they gave me five of these. As a result of that present of five cattleyas, I realized that orchids could be grown without the aid of a greenhouse, and the seeds were sown for the enthusiastic creation of a fairly large and varied collection.

For the next two years I grew orchids, until my collection filled every window-

sill in my apartment. The window in my large bathroom, which has an eastern exposure, became crammed full of plants. Eventually, the entire bathroom was filled to capacity with standing lights, small humidifiers and plants on tiered trays, hanging from curtain rods and even in the bathtub. At this time I began experimenting with growing orchids in flasks and community pots, which I had bought from commercial growers. By then there were nearly 300 plants in the bathroom. The time had come to expand. The next couple of months were spent corresponding and telephoning suppliers and tradespeople. My "indoor greenhouse" began taking shape.

I decided to use my living room, which is 20 by 30 feet, for my growing area. My apartment is on the 12th floor of a building in Manhattan. First, I had the walls, ceiling and window trim painted with two coats of an epoxy moisture-proof paint containing a fungicide. I then installed a fiberglass-reinforced plastic floor. The periphery of the room was ramped using feathered 2x4 lum-

ber, and a polyethylene (.004-.005 gauge) sheet was laid to cover and protect the existing wooden floor. Then $\frac{1}{8}$-inch-thick brown fiberglass panels were installed and seamed to contain water or fertilizer. Also connected to the plumbing is a line for my standard Engineering Humidifier Model 37.

The next major step was lighting. Galen Lee, who I first met on my trips to the monthly AOS regional judgings at the New York Botanical Garden, was very helpful in advising and assisting me in setting up this room. He participated in my conversations with the Agronomics Department of the GTE Sylvania Company. On the basis of these conversations, I decided to order two steel-framed tables made to my measurements by a division of GTE Sylvania.

Each table is 12 feet long by 5 feet wide and consists of two levels. The first or bottom level is 12 inches off the floor, while the top or upper growing area of the table is 34 inches off the floor. The long sides of the tables are parallel to each other, with a 2-foot aisle between

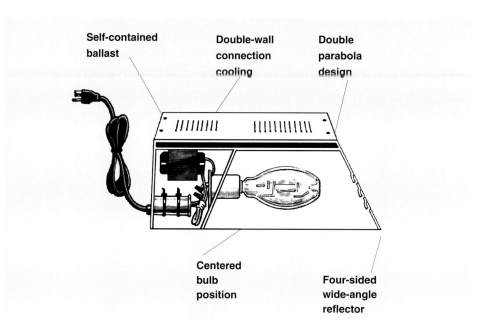

Self-contained ballast

Double-wall connection cooling

Double parabola design

Centered bulb position

Four-sided wide-angle reflector

the two. Thus the tables are set up to be, together, a 12-foot square. Centered at the ends of each table is a square pole that is 9½ feet high from the floor. The pole supports a cross-beam at that height above the top of the table.

From each of these two beams running the 12-foot length of the tables, hang two large reflectors. Each reflector houses a 1,000-watt high-pressure-sodium bulb: the GTE Sylvania Maxi-Gro B luminaries.

I covered the two growing levels with ³/₄-inch plywood boards. Together with liquid fiberglass the final effect was that I had a solid fiberglass shell on the table.

Next came the installation of a double-basin sink with a large counter. The corner of the room where this was installed was to be the center for potting and for my water supply. I have a 50-foot ³/₈-inch plastic hose attached to the pipes under the sink with a water wand on the end, to which I can attach a regular water head, a rosette, or a fine-mist sprayer. I also have a Merit Commander fertilizer proportioner attached under the sink and, depending on which faucet I

Opposite: The Hydrofarm fixture for 400-watt metal-halide HID lamps has a remote ballast connected to the lamp socket (left) by an 8-foot-long grounded cord. With a heavy ballast removed from the lamp reflector, it is easier to arrange safe placement of both components. This type of two-part HID unit accepts either halide or sodium lamps in 400- and 1,000-watt sizes. A lightweight reflector and lamp design (about 15 pounds) like this is suitable for mounting on moving light tracts or rotating Sun Circles to spread light evenly around the growing area.
Above: Smaller HID lamps (150 to 400 watts) can be used in a fixture that contains the ballast, socket and reflector in a single unit. The Sunburst Grow light can accept lamps up to 400 watts, plug into standard three-hole grounded outlets and is designed to hang from metal chains above the plants.

turn on, I can add dilute fertilizer to the running water.

The electricians spent the next week installing electrical capacity for the growing area, wiring and hanging the four large 1,000-watt lights from the beams above the tables and installing four rows of fluorescent lamps, each lamp with four tubes running 12 feet (8-foot and 4-foot fixtures) and attached to the bottom of the plywood covering the upper level of the bench.

1,000 Watt Systems

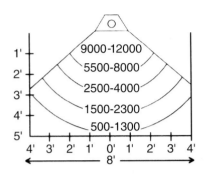

400 Watt Systems

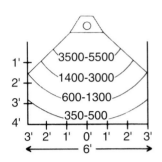

250 Watt Systems

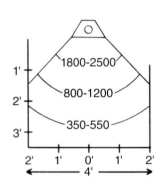

150 and 175 Watt Systems

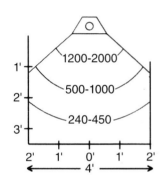

This gave us a light bank of 16 fluorescent tubes — alternating warm- and cool-white — across the top of the lower growing area of each of the two tables. The four large 1,000-watt bulbs are sufficient light for the upper-level growing area. The heavy ballasts for these large overhanging bulbs rest on a window bench, and throw off amazingly little heat. The ballasts for the fluorescent tubes are a much greater source of heat.

One of the mistakes I made in this design led to unnecessary light intensity and extra heat produced by the fluorescent tubes that light the lower shelves. Now, instead of 16 tubes on at any one time, I usually use only 10 or 12. Three strips (four tubes per strip) rather than four would have been all I needed.

Above: These drawings show approximate foot-candles at various distances for specific HID lamps. Foot-candle readings can vary greatly due to ambient light levels, age of the bulb and the light meter. Useful light intensity can be increased by using light movers, placing multiple fixtures in each growing area and by attaching reflective materials to nearby surfaces such as walls.

Seven large fans located around the room and a series of small "muffin" fans attached at various points along the beams of the tables circulate the air as well as remove the heat from the fluorescent light ballasts over the lower growing area. The large Standard Engineering humidifier is mounted on a stand about 6 feet high at one end of the aisle between the tables, and at the other end, sitting on the floor, is a 6-gallon Holland humidifier with fan enclosed. The pool

for the Holland humidifier is manually cleaned and filled with water twice a week. At the same end of the table as this portable humidifier is a large wooden frame resting on the top ends of the two tables and anchored to the tall poles at that end. This frame encloses a solid piece

Top: Artificial lighting turned an unused space into a growing area in the former apartment of Robert Weltz, Jr. High-intensity sodium lights are above the benches, while fluorescent lamps hang below. The repotting area, water source and a humidifier are to the right

Above: Compact orchids with cool-growing needs thrive under fluorescent lights, while orchids needing brighter light and more heat live above.

Growing Orchids Under Lights

of chicken wire about 12 feet long by 5 feet high on which I hang a multitude of orchids mounted on cork, tree fern or branches.

On the top of each of the upper and lower growing areas of each table, sitting on the plywood boards, are six stainless-steel pans that each measure 5 feet by 2 feet by about 2 inches deep, for a total of 24 such containers. Each pan has square, stainless-steel tubes along its sides to support plastic egg crates or louver sheets on which the potted plants stand. Each tray has a hole and a funnel-like removable plug so that when the plants are watered the water runs into and fills the pans to a level of about $1\frac{1}{4}$ inches. When this level is exceeded, the excess water drains through the hoses into pails on the floor, thus providing a practical way of watering, as well as creating extra humidity under the plants in the room. The trays are easily cleaned about once a year by pulling the steel plugs and hosing down the inside of the trays without removing the plants. I put wooden wedges between the trays and the plywood boards at this time to facilitate water flow, and then I refill the trays with fresh water and about an ounce of Physan (an algicide and fungicide) per tray. R·D·20 is a similar liquid product.

The lights and large humidifier all work automatically, and during the winter months are on from about 7 am to 6:30 pm. As the days lengthen from spring into summer, the lights and humidifier are adjusted gradually to stay on nearly two hours longer. The fans operate 24 hours a day, all year long. The temperature is very primitively controlled by manually opening and closing three of the six windows on the north and east sides of the room. During the four or five coldest months of the year, the windows at night might be closed completely or opened only an inch.

No heat is ever used in the room. Night temperatures during the cold

weather are maintained at 58 to 60 F in this manner, while during the day, with the windows opened wider, the temperature rises to 70 to 75 F due to the heat released from all the operating lights.

During the warm weather, from about April to October, a large air conditioner operates on a thermostat, and three windows are left open. The night temperature during this time is about 65 F and the day temperatures range from 80 to 90 F, rarely hotter. I keep adjustable screens on the insides of the windows, otherwise the room would be full of bees and large flies all spring and summer.

I grow most of my plants in clay pots and I vary the watering and fertilizing schedule according to genus and plant size. My collection now numbers nearly 3,000 plants, ranging from many specimen-size plants to tiny seedlings.

Eventually, I added additional growing space to my indoor greenhouse by building storage cabinets 4 feet high along the 20-foot interior west wall. On top of these cabinets I have a long, narrow area measuring 16 feet long and $2\frac{1}{2}$ feet wide. Over

this growing area I have two strips, hanging end to end, of 8-foot UHO (ultra-high output) fluorescent tubes. Each strip has one warm-white and one cool-white tube with recessed pins. These lights are very suitable for my paphiopedilums, plants in community pots and small seedlings.

The big sodium lamps seem to be very effective for most genera. The only notable exceptions are the paphiopedilums, which I have in great profusion. They do not seem to like the light intensity of the big bulbs. On the other hand, my phalaenopsis, which are supposed to have the same light requirements as paphiopedilums, do well under the sodium lights, and, I presume, have adjusted to them. Miltonias and other members of the *Oncidium* Alliance grow particularly well and put out very large, strong and heavily flowered spikes under the sodium lights. The *Cattleya* Alliance (epidendrums, cattleyas and laelias) also seems to do very well, as do my ascocendas, angraecums, lycastes and a pair of ansellias that are growing so rapidly they are about to take over the room.

Opposite: A sodium lamp casts light onto a *Vanda* hybrid in the former New York City apartment of Robert Weltz Jr.
Above: A small muffin fan positioned beneath the top bench circulates air 24 hours a day.

The sodium bulbs have not been changed since they were installed. I was told that they have a life of upwards of 25,000 to 30,000 light hours. The fluorescent tubes are changed about every 12 months.

Although few plants flower in summer, by late October, many orchids are in flower, including large numbers of *Paphiopedilum* species and hybrids, *Dendrobium phalaenopsis* hybrids, *Lycaste* hybrids, *Laelia* species, ascocendas, *Catasetum* species, *Oncidium* species and hybrids, *Epidendrum ilense*, *Ansellia africana*, *Phragmipedium* species and hybrids, assorted pleurothallids and numerous cattleyas and phalaenopsis.

A System of Moving Lights
Another successful AOS light gardener is real-estate appraiser Kenneth M.

Rossman, who grows orchids under a combination of metal-halide and high-pressure-sodium tubes. To increase the useful growing area he uses motors to move lamps, thus throwing light around. Rossman uses a light mover that rolls the fixture back and forth along a 4-, 6- or 8-foot-long rail. By using two lights end to end he can extend the rail up to 16 feet, or make a circular light pattern. A light mover reduces heat cast from the tubes because the lamps are kept moving. A vanda can be grown 4 inches away from HID lamps if grown under moving fixtures, while the same lamps would need to be 24 to 30 inches away if they were kept stationary.

According to Rossman, to construct a moderate starter setup that will adequately cover a 10x10-foot growing area, assemble these supplies:

■ A 400- to 1,000-watt metal halide fixture with ballast ($200-$400).
■ A high-pressure-sodium fixture with ballast ($200-$400).
■ A light mover (8-foot ganged and motorized rail or Sun Circle) ($150-$300).

■ Two heavy-duty grounded timers ($50-$80).
■ Humidifier, preferably with a humidistat and plumbed into your water source ($150-$300).
■ At least two large fans ($70-$160).
■ Two growing benches ($200-$400).
■ Light meter ($25-$50).
■ Minimum-maximum thermometer ($20-$50).
■ Humidity gauge and hygrometer ($10-$30).

An initial investment of US$1,000 for this type of setup is realistic. These lights operate on 110-volt current and should be on their own circuit. Anyone lacking electrical expertise is encouraged to hire an electrician to make the necessary modifications.

Grower Rossman has success giving his orchids the same number of light hours as outdoors. This ranges from 11 hours in the winter at his New York home to 18 hours in the summer. Every two weeks, the timer is adjusted at 15-minute increments to make sure the right amount of light is provided to the plants.

Growing Orchids Under Lights

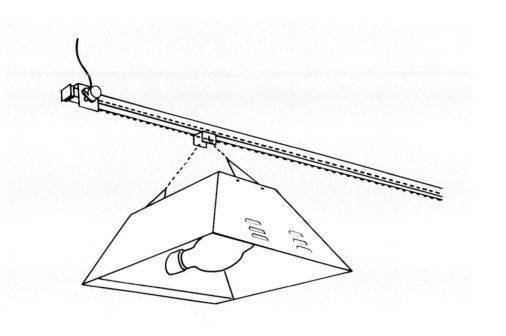

Cultural Advice

In the Rossman collection, there is a 15 to 20 F differential between day and night temperatures. Ventilation is from skylights and open doors plus three wall-mounted fans that operate continuously. Humidity is maintained by a direct-plumbed Herrmidifier 500 humidifier controlled by a humidistat set at 70 percent.

From late April or early May (spring-time in New York) until October, Rossman puts most of his orchids out-doors, a procedure followed by many orchid growers in temperate climates. Some of the orchids grown successfully by Rossman and other light gardeners are: *Angraecum leonis*, *Bulbophyllum lobbii*, *Cattleya* hybrids, *Dendrobium cuthbertsonii*, *Dendrobium* hybrids such as *Den.* Kalagas, *Den.* Pixie Princess and *Den.* Precious Pearl, *Encyclia* species, *Oncidium* species and hybrids, *Paphiopedilum* species and hybrids, *Phalaenopsis* hybrids and *Vanda* hybrids.

High-intensity-discharge lamps are most useful in vacant rooms, basements and other areas where you wish to grow

Opposite left: Ascocentrum curvifolium is among the high-light orchids suitable for growing under high-intensity lamps. This Old World native, which can be grown in a container or a slat basket, requires warm temperatures.
Opposite right: Placing containers on a plastic grid permits water to drain rapidly. A tray below catches the water.
Above: The Hydrofarm Light Track uses a lifetime-lubricated motor to slowly move an HID lamp back and forth along a length of metal track. Every 20 minutes, the fixture will travel about 6 feet and then return and repeat the process.

orchids, but will not spend much time. However, although fluorescent lamps are more practical in living rooms and places where you will linger for hours, new features of high-intensity lamps and fixtures make them worth considering for any part of the home.

Attractive wall units equipped with high-intensity lamps that blend into a diversity of decors are one option. Another is multiple-shelf garden carts that increase the growing area and allow the homeowner to install a combination of lights, perhaps hanging fluorescent lamps on one level and high-intensity lamps on the other.

8 ~ Culture Basics

ORCHIDS WERE THE FIRST tropicals I grew under lights more than 35 years ago and they grew so well that fluorescents have become a permanent feature of my indoor growing systems. Success with orchids under lights begins when you select species and hybrids suited to the conditions you can provide.

Moderate to Strong Light

If you plan to grow orchids in a bookshelf garden where moderate light is provided by two broad-spectrum lamps, select moth orchids (*Phalaenopsis*) or lady's-slipper orchids (*Paphiopedilum*), genera that thrive under medium light. If you want to grow ascocendas, cattleya-type hybrids or bulbous epidendrums totally under fluorescents, the light must be strong, as furnished by three or more 40-watt broad-spectrum lamps.

Some members of the American Orchid Society have experimented for years with fluorescents, many growing orchids in bright growth chambers or plant rooms.

Del Hollenberg, for example, built a cabinet, painted it white inside, and installed banks of fluorescents three inches apart to provide a flood of light for cattleya hybrids. In fact, the intensity was so strong that his phalaenopsis had to be shaded or placed to the sides where light falls off.

In my own collection, many genera thrive under four 40-watt broad-spectrum lamps. In the greenhouse, where orchids receive some direct sun in the morning but only diffuse light after noon, I provide supplemental fluorescent light with two 40-watt lamps hung about 10 inches above the foliage. Some of my cattleya hybrids make growths under the medium light of only two lamps, yet produce satisfactory flowers. However, for certain bloom on a wide range of hybrids, I find fixtures with four lamps are better.

Light-Hour Variations

Most species are day-neutral and bloom well with 13 to 14 light-hours per period. A few must have precise combinations of light or temperature changes to bloom freely. In the tropics, orchids experience little change between night- and day-length. Species along the equator live with 12-hour days all year. Those in mountainous regions can still experience 15- to 60-minute variations between day and night according to season and topography. Although the official sunset may come at 6 pm, orchids on a tree branch in the valley may be quite dark by 5 pm.

If you have a collection of mature orchids from several genera, vary the light-hours slightly according to the season. Provide 16 to 18 hours of light from spring into late summer.

In September, reduce daylength to 14 hours, then to 12 hours November through January. As the year progresses, gradually increase the light to 16 hours by March or early April. This program will assure bloom on species that require a light-duration change for flower-bud initiation.

Phalaenopsis amabilis, the white moth orchid, when grown with long nights at 65 F minimum night temperature, will often bloom more than once a year. With short nights, blooming is reduced to once a year. A similar reaction to long nights occurs with the pink moth orchid, *Phalaenopsis schilleriana,* and in *Dendrobium phalaenopsis*, an Asian species with round flowers resembling those of the moth orchids.

Night Temperatures

Night temperatures no higher than 65 F are important for maximum flowering, since warmer nights inhibit bloom, regardless of night length. This is especially

true for species from high altitudes and during the autumn when many orchids are initiating buds. Tests to determine the complex interrelationships between temperature and dark periods have yet to be conducted with most orchids.

However, we do know that *Cattleya warscewiczii* and *Cattleya gaskelliana*, both large-flowered species that bloom as new growth matures, require long nights at 55 F for maximum bloom. *Cattleya labiata*, an autumn-flowering species that is in the background of many hybrids, also needs 13-hour nights to initiate flowers, but temperatures are not so crucial and 60 to 65 F nights are satisfactory.

Commercial Controls

Commercial growers capitalize on these reactions to achieve maximum bloom for Christmas, Easter and Mother's Day. To hold back bloom on winter-flowering hybrids so as to have flowers for Easter, a grower would turn on lights for two to three extra hours of "day" in autumn and winter.

Above: A key ingredient to growing healthy orchids is choosing the right potting medium. Several are available for orchids, among them hard osmunda, cork slabs, tree-fern chunks, soft osmunda, redwood bark and ground tree-fern fiber.

Lights might burn from 5:30 am to 7:30 am (sunrise), thus tricking plants into holding back bloom. To encourage flowering, stop extending the days and the plants will flower in about four months. Such commercial controls are impractical for a home collection.

Modern cattleyas and other popular orchids are often complex hybrids with several species or even different genera in their makeup, and these hybrids are not so predictable in their light-period reactions. Fortunately, most of the orchids you are likely to grow will thrive without special manipulation of light hours.

A nursery in Vashon, Washington, reports that most of the firm's yellow, green and art-shade cattleya hybrids bloom in summer as long-day plants. In my collection, I have some new hybrids involving *Cattleya, Laelia, Brassavola*

Growing Orchids Under Lights

and *Sophronitis* producing plants with yellow to red-bronze flowers. These appear without fail every summer. Growths are made under the long days and short nights of spring and summer.

Another example is the butterfly-shaped *Oncidium* Kalihi (*kramerianum* x *papilio*), a favorite for its habit of flowering on and off throughout the year. A clump of this yellow-and-brown hybrid has grown for four years on a bright living room windowsill. It receives supplemental light from an overhead fluorescent that provides little intensity because I use it mainly to illuminate flowers at night. However, a side effect is that this orchid has had short nights all year round. Little intensity is required for plants to react as though it were still daytime. Unlike some of the pure cattleyas, which need slightly longer nights than days to bloom, this oncidium hybrid has been a joy, producing one golden-and-brown ruffle-edged butterfly after another on long thin spikes.

Faster Bloom

Seedling orchids grow faster under extended days. Zuma Canyon Orchids in Malibu, California, employs artificial light over seedlings to extend days to 18 light hours. Seedlings make four months' growth in three months' time, thanks to the supplemental light. Homeowners can use a similar program to extend days and raise light levels without risk of burning seedlings, as might occur with sunshine.

Since orchids may take five to six years to bloom from seed, any means of accelerating growth is valuable. Provide up to 18-hour days until plants reach maturity, then follow the schedule given for mature plants. Autumn and winter long nights, with 60 to 65 F temperatures, prompt mature seedlings to bloom. Using lights to speed orchid seedlings to maturity is especially useful in temperate zones where the sunlight is weaker and of shorter duration in the winter.

Culture Basics

Epiphytes Orchids such as cattleyas and phalaenopsis normally live on tree branches or mossy rocks in the tropics. These are epiphytic genera and require an airy compost. Mixtures of tree bark (fir or redwood), coarse perlite and tree-fern fibers are easiest to use, although some growers still pot in osmunda, a tough fern root. Commercial orchid growers sell ready-mixed orchid potting mixes and the various ingredients, too. Pot epiphytes in relatively small pots with at least 1 inch of gravel or crock for drainage. Burn extra holes in plastic pots. Some growers use plastic foam "peanuts" as drainage material. Orchid roots often grow around and into these chunks.

Terrestrials Some orchids grow best with an airy humus-rich compost containing soil. Species that live with rotted leaves around their roots, as in a tree crotch or on the forest floor, should be potted in a well-drained terrestrial-orchid compost that stays slightly moist. These terrestrial growers, including *Cymbidium* and *Paphiopedilum*, can actually

Growing Orchids Under Lights

be potted in modified humus-rich soil, but should not be grown in straight soil as used for a geranium or other fully terrestrial houseplants. Mixtures of chopped sphagnum moss, pasteurized loam and tree barks are satisfactory and such mixes are offered ready-made by many dealers.

Humidity A minimum humidity of 50 to 60 percent is necessary to keep orchids healthy. This moisture in the air can be furnished by growing plants in groups over moist gravel or perlite and by using a humidifier.

Watering Epiphytic orchids, such as cattleyas, epidendrums and oncidiums, often have swollen stems called pseudobulbs that store moisture. In the wild, during dry seasons, they go weeks without water, kept alive by the stored moisture and light evening dews or mists.

Such species can go a week or more without water if humidity is maintained at 50 percent. Other epiphytes, such as the moth orchids (*Phalaenopsis*), have no pseudobulbs so they must be kept evenly moist with only slight drying of the medium between soakings.

Opposite: Consider use of a portable humidifier where humidity is low in the home.
Above: Lights can increase growing space in the greenhouse, too. Here, Vita Lite Powertwist and Cool White fluorescents placed beneath a bench in a greenhouse supplement natural light to create a growing area.

In no event must epiphytic orchids be kept soggy. It is always better to let the roots dry slightly between waterings. Potting mixes of bark, perlite and tree fern drain quickly when used above adequate crocks or gravel. Containers made for orchids have extra drainage holes in them. Terrestrial orchids do well when kept evenly moist. Soak the medium but then let it dry slightly before watering again.

Fertilizing Provide a slow-release balanced fertilizer (14-14-14) for orchids under lights as insurance against underfertilizing. Plants in bark will need some extra nitrogen, as in a 30-10-10 water-soluble formula. Substitute a low-nitrogen formula when plants have completed new growth to encourage bloom rather than continued vegetative growth. Apply no extra fertilizer to orchids that are resting — that is, not making new growth.

Growing Orchids Under Lights

9 ~ Propagating Orchids

ORCHIDS ARE REMARKABLY EASY to propagate so you can share your collection with friends or trade divisions for new additions to your collection. After you've grown orchids for a year or two, some of your plants may have outgrown their containers and will require repotting. Often this is also an ideal time to divide a specimen.

Species with pseudobulbs, such as cattleyas and lycastes, need at least two to four growths (three to five is better) per clump. Divide potbound specimens when roots begin to emerge; if the roots grow too long before a plant is divided, they may snap off and reduce the plant's ability to root. Cut through the rhizome with a sterile knife or precision shears. Dust the cut with a fungicide and root-stimulating powder such as Rootone and then pot. Sterilize the cutting tool between use on each plant. Lay a stack of newspapers on the potting area and remove a sheet after repotting or dividing each plant.

This will help prevent the spread of virus. Pot each division in the new container at the same level it was in the old container. A wire support that clips onto the edge of the container may help stabilize the division, which is important to help roots anchor themselves.

Orchids without pseudobulbs may produce plantlets on old inflorescences or alongside the main crown. These are called "keikis," a Hawaiian term meaning baby plant. Remove plantlets once they have roots several inches long or let them remain with the large plant for a clump effect.

New hybrids and select species are propagated by seed sown on nutrient agar or by a modern vegetative process called meristemming. Here, a portion of the growing point is cut out of the rhizome and then this speck of tissue is cultured on nutrient agar in a flask (that creates a sterile environment). This process, called meristem propagation, provides thousands of plantlets genetically identical to the parent plant. Commercial dealers offer meristem plantlets of fine, often awarded, orchids at prices close to that of unbloomed seedlings. Before meristem propagation, divisions of the same orchids sold for hundreds of dollars. When purchasing meristems of awarded orchids, make certain the label has the clonal name plus the award designation.

Experienced growers may opt to expand their collections through the purchase of seedlings. Many nurseries sell compots — a small pot with several seedlings. This offers growers the opportunity to increase their orchid collection at a reasonable cost and have extra plants they can share with friends and trade for new additions to their collections. When purchasing a compot, make sure the seedlings are well rooted and the leaf color is a reflection of proper culture.

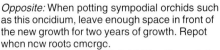

Opposite: When potting sympodial orchids such as this oncidium, leave enough space in front of the new growth for two years of growth. Repot when new roots emerge.
Top: This *Phalaenopsis* hybrid (Eye Dee x Spica) produces an abundance of plantlets that can be removed and potted to get more plants to trade

with friends or donate to an orchid club's plant table or raffle.
Above left: Phalaenopsis compots under fluorescent lamps, which receive 10 hours of light every 24 hours, increase a collection at low cost.
Above: Cool-White fluorescent bulbs give bright light without danger of burning orchid seedlings.

Growing Orchids Under Lights

10 ~ Growing Healthy Orchids

YOUR ORCHIDS WILL SELDOM suffer from pests or disease if you use clean, fresh potting media, maintain air circulation and isolate new arrivals until it is known they harbor no harmful organisms. Normal biological occurrences, such as yellowing of lower foliage, frighten some people into thinking the worst. However, most foliage troubles are due either to the normal falling of older leaves or improper environmental conditions, rather than pests or disease.

Healthy roots are necessary for attractive foliage and flowers. Overwatering, extreme binding of roots due to being in the same container too long, and extreme drying can all kill roots. With injured roots a plant begins to cut down on above-ground demands, mainly by slowing top growth and losing leaves.

Hot and dry conditions may cause leaves to get brown edges. Soaking the roots does not completely compensate for lack of moisture in the air. Therefore, strive to maintain a minimum of 50 to 60 percent humidity where you wish to have healthy orchids.

Cold water or too strong fertilizer will cause leaves to develop brown spots. Water plants with room-temperature water. Fertilizers are safe in solution but only when mixed according to directions or weaker. Some insecticides may also cause foliage damage but without causing permanent harm. Make sure any insecticide is approved for use on orchids and mix and apply following the manufacturer's directions. Apply sprays only where there is adequate ventilation.

Treatment for Pests

Wash off any pests you find. Use lukewarm water in a fairly strong stream to dislodge them and wash them down the drain. A mist of rubbing alcohol will also control most pests by killing them directly. Although alcohol does not kill most insect eggs, it is easy to apply and subdues adult insects. Then for complete protection, spray with an insecticide (ask your local orchid nursery or a member of an orchid society for a recommendation).

Follow directions carefully. Too much insecticide will harm plants; too little will permit pests to build up a resistance.

Add several drops of fish emulsion per gallon of spray solution to help the chemical stick on foliage. If you choose to use aerosol sprays, be sure to hold the can 2 to 3 feet away and let only the mist fall on the leaves. Apply insecticides and fungicides when temperatures are between 70 and 80 F. Some sprays will cause foliage injury if applied when temperatures are above 85 F.

Avoid getting spray on the lamps unless you plan to clean the glass later with a damp cloth. Accumulations of spray reduce light output. One spraying rarely kills all pests because eggs may hatch later. Therefore, eight to 10 days after the first application, use the spray again. If a heavy infestation of pests or bad fungus attack occurs, isolate the affected plants until they are clean again. These are the most common houseplant pests:

Aphids Sucking insects that cluster on new shoots and flower buds where they reproduce at a startling rate. Aphids may be brown or green and can be seen without a magnifying glass.

Mealybugs These are cottonlike sucking pests that cluster in new growth and between stems and leaves. Remove all you can by washing with soapy water, then wipe the infected areas with rubbing alcohol. Severe infestations require the application of an insecticide.

Red Spider Mites These red-green mites first attack the undersides of foliage. Heavy infestations turn leaves yellow; fine webs will be seen. Light infes-

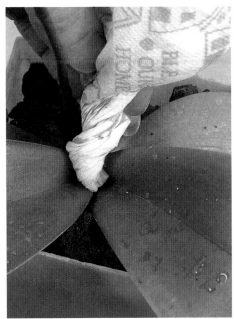

tations are best identified with a magnifying glass, which will reveal the tiny moving mites on the undersurfaces of leaves. These pests thrive in dry places so misting leaves underneath will discourage but not kill them.

Scale Scales look like small lumps of sap or wax on stems or leaf veins. Some species are white, others dark brown, but all are dangerous for plants because they suck away nutrients. Gently scrub off all the scales; an old soft-bristled toothbrush and soapy water will do the job. Then apply an all-purpose spray.

Slugs and Snails These pests eat leaves, buds and stems. Maintain a clean collection so snails and slugs will have no place to hide. Spread slug pellets or drench with a chemical made specifically to control slugs and snails.

Thrips These minute insects damage buds, especially on plants in the *Vanda* Alliance, causing them not to open. Thrips may also spread bacteria, fungi and viruses. Diazinon or malathion should give adequate control.

Above left: An oscillating fan will provide adequate air movement to help keep orchids healthy.
Above: To prevent disease in phalaenopsis, use paper towel to absorb standing water from the plant's crown.

Diseases

Disease is seldom a problem but from time to time a fungus may attack weak plants or rot cause a too-moist plant to die back. The ultimate cure is adequate spacing of plants, moving air and dry foliage at night.

Algae

Algae can cause gravel or perlite in light-garden trays to turn green and thus reduce light for the plants. An excellent control for algae that is also safe for plants is Physan 20 (R·D·20 is similar). This is a clear liquid that is mixed at 1 teaspoon per gallon of water to spray on seedlings or over pot tops to prevent growth of algae and some forms of fungi. At a stronger dilution (1 tablespoon per gallon), it will sanitize containers. The weaker dilution is recommended for algae control if it is applied monthly.

Growing Orchids Under Lights

11 ~ Gallery of Genera

THE FOLLOWING ORCHIDS ARE well suited to culture in light gardens. Unless noted, they are adaptable to intermediate temperatures (60 to 65 F nights). Especially good results can be obtained by supplementing sunlight with broad-spectrum fluorescent lamps, but even with no daylight, these orchids will prove rewarding under lights.

In the descriptions below, the genus name is followed by pronunciation for the genus name and then the recommended distance between lamps and plants is given.

Aerangis
(air-RANG-iss)
6" to 8"

These are mainly dwarf monopodial (single-crown) epiphytes from Africa and nearby islands in the Indian Ocean. *Aerangis biloba* grows 3 to 5 inches, and has 1-inch waxy, white fragrant flowers. *Aerangis compacta*, a similar species, can

be grown on a small coffee tree just as it is found in Uganda. *Aerangis luteo-alba* Var. *rhodosticta* may reach 6 inches and has sprays of long-spurred white flowers with red centers. Provide 65 to 68 F nights.

Amesiella
(aymes-ee-EL-ah)
4" to 6"

There is only one species in this genus — *Amesiella philippinensis*. Once classified as an *Angraecum*, this miniature orchid bears pristine white fragrant flowers with a long spur.

Angraecum
(an-GREY-kum)
4" to 6"

Night-fragrant, white-flowered epiphytes from the same habitat as *Aerangis*, the angraecums offer more diversity. The angraecums bloom mainly in winter on 1- to 3-foot-tall plants, which can be somewhat tall for a light garden. *Angraecum magdalenae* is a dwarf, 6- to 8-inch-tall plant, so hybrids with this smaller species and the popular large-flowered angraecums should produce some compact gems.

Ascocentrum
(ass-koh-SEN-trum)
2" to 6"

Dwarf orange, yellow, red, or rose-flowered epiphytes from tropical Asia, ascocentrums do best when they receive some sunlight or are grown beneath strong broad-spectrum fluorescents. Hybrids with *Vanda*, called *Ascocenda*, have an adaptable nature and compact 8- to 15-inch-tall stems; they bloom several times a year when provided with 65 to 68 F nights. Hybridizers have combined *Ascocentrum* with *Doritis*, a dwarf *Phalaenopsis* relative, to produce some compact hybrids — *Doricentrum* — that thrive under lights.

Opposite: Angraecum Compactolena 'Talisman Cove', a cross between *Angcm. compactum* and *Angcm. magdalenae*, grows well under lights. *Top:* Hybrids between *Ascocentrum* and *Vanda* are often compact and floriferous. One choice: *Ascocenda* Silpapraset (*V.* Rothschildiana x *Ascda.* Aroonsri Beauty).

Above left: Complex hybrids in the *Vanda* Alliance, including *Doricentrum* Pulcherrimin (*Doritis pulcherrima* x *Ascocentrum miniatum*), offer possibilities for under-lights culture. *Above: Rhynchocentrum* Lilac Blossom (*Rhy. coelestis* x *Asctm. ampullaceum*) bears $^3/_4$-inch flowers on a 6-inch-tall plant.

Aspasia
(ass-PAY-zee-ah)
4" to 6"

Fragrant waxy yellow, brown, and white long-lasting flowers are trademarks of these compact epiphytes that grow 6 to 8 inches tall. Try *Aspasia principissa*, a native of Panama that flowers in the spring. *Brapasia* Serene, a hybrid between *Asp. principissa* and *Brassia gireoudiana* (a spider orchid), bears fragrant 4-inch yellow flowers.

Brassavola
(brah-SAH-voh-lah)
2" to 6"

Central and South America are home to these adaptable epiphytes, which are tolerant of low humidity. Species *Brassavola nodosa*, called lady-of-the-night for its nocturnally fragrant white flowers, typically grows in strong sunlight but adapts to light culture and responds with several flushes of bloom per year. Hybrids of *B. nodosa* crossed with *Cattleya* or *Laelia* inherit the compact, close-growing habit, and often make fine

Above left: Brapasia Serene 'Talisman Cove' bears 4-inch fragrant flowers.
Above: Compact-growing *Odontobrassia* Kenneth Bivin 'Santa Barbara' (*Odontoglossum cariniferum* x *Brassia longissima*) thrives in intermediate temperatures (60 to 68 F).

hybrids for the light garden. Another benefit — increased color options.

Brassia
(BRASS-ee-ah)
6" to 8"

Brassias (spider orchids) are epiphytes with yellow flowers, spotted brown, each having long spidery tepals (petals and sepals that are indistinguishable). *Brassia maculata* from Jamaica and Central America has sprays of fragrant yellow-cream, 5- to 8-inch flowers dotted maroon. Brassia Edvah Loo (*longissima* x *gireoudiana*), puts forth 8- to 10-inch-long flowers in spring and autumn.

Catasetum
(kat-ah-SEE-tum)
4" to 6"

From Latin America come these un-

Top: The fragrant flowers of *Brassavola nodosa*, which perfume the air early in the evening, give rise to the species' common name of lady-of-the-night orchid. *Brassavola nodosa* has been used in many hybrids that expand the variety of colors and patterns available to the light-garden grower. The species flowers several times a year.

Above left: Catasetums satisfy those with an appetite for unusual flowers. Among the many hybrids is this *Catasetum* Lovena (*fimbriatum* x Susan Fuchs), which bears fragrant flowers on a compact plant.
Above: Catasetum Coromandel is a cross between *Cstm. fimbriatum* and *Ctsm. maculatum.*

usual epiphytes with fragrant, waxy flowers, which are usually either male or female but occasionally perfect (bisexual). Pot catasetums in small containers filled with a porous mix of tree fern or bark mix. Provide the plants with 65 to 68 F nights. When the pseudobulbs stop producing leaves, gradually withhold water. Leaves will begin to fall as plants enter their four- to eight-week resting period. *Catasetum pileatum*, the national flower of Venezuela, has 3- to 4-inch, yellow-to-white, wide-lipped flowers in the autumn. *Catasetum warscewiczii* is a 3- to 4-inch dwarf plant with a pendulous inflorescence on which many 1¹/₂-inch greenish-white flowers are borne. Recent hybrids are exciting and adaptable. Look for *Catasetum* Francis Nelson (*trulla* x *fimbriatum*) and *Catasetum* Orchidglade (*pileatum* x *expansum*). This genus responds well to regular applications of fertilizer on a weekly basis when new growths are being made. Mix ¹/₂ teaspoon of organic fish emulsion in each gallon of balanced-chemical fertilizer for catasetums making rapid growth.

Cattleya
(KAT-lee-ah)
3" to 6"

These traditional corsage orchids often reach 2 to 3 feet in height, but with careful selection, you can obtain compact species and their hybrids that bloom when only 8 to 12 inches tall. Such hybrids are offered as "mini-catts" in several catalogs, and they are also often sold at nurseries and at orchid shows. All cattleyas are epiphytes with swollen pseudobulbs and thick white roots. Bright light is required for maximum bloom. Compact types include:

Cattleya aclandiae, a Brazilian species with fragrant 3- to 4-inch flowers, which are borne on a 4- to 5-inch-tall plant.

Cattleya aurantiaca from Mexico and Central America has bright orange flowers in clusters, a characteristic passed on to its hybrids such as the rewarding *Laeliocattleya* Chit Chat 'Tangerine' (*Lc.* Coronet x *aurantiaca*).

Cattleya forbesii is a slender 10- to 12-inch-tall plant from Brazil. Its flowers are yellow with dark-brown markings.

Primary hybrids of this species do well under lights. Among the choices are *Laeliocattleya* Forphylla (*forbesii* x *harpophylla*) and *Laeliocattleya* Little Lemon Drops (*forbesii* x *briegeri*).

Cattleya intermedia, a spring-and-summer-blooming species from Brazil, has waxy lavender flowers in clusters, splashed petals (var. *aquinii*) or white with colored lip types.

Cattleya walkeriana has 3- to 5-inch stems but large 3- to 4-inch fragrant rose or white flowers. Its hybrids are compact, too. *Cattleya walkeriana* blooms mainly in winter.

The majority of cattleya species and their hybrids will produce maximum bloom under four to eight broad-spectrum lamps (such as Wide-Spectrum Gro-Lux) or with a combination of sunlight and fluorescents. Hybrids with *Sophronitis* are generally free-flowering and somewhat more compact than pure cattleya or laeliocattleya hybrids.

Excellent mericlones with compact habit include *Sophrolaeliocattleya* Madge Fordyce 'Red Orb' (red, winter

Opposite left: Laeliocattleya Angel Heart (Puppy Love x *Cattleya* Penny Kuroda) is a compact hybrid with long-lasting flowers. This plant was grown under broad-spectrum fluorescent lamps. *Opposite right:* Fragrant flowers and a compact habit combine in this *Cattleya* hybrid (Acker's Lovely x *interglossa*). *Above left:* Fluorescent lamps coax a show of lovely flowers from this *Cattleya* hybrid (Jungle Spots x *amethystoglossa*), a compact plant with fragrant flowers. *Above: Cattleya* Small World (*aclandiae* x *luteola*).

to spring) and *Sophrolaeliocattleya* Jewel Box 'Crimson Glory' (red flowers, winter to spring).

Comparettia
(kom-pah-RET-ee-ah)
3" to 8"

Comparettia macroplectron is an epiphyte native to Colombia. Although it is only 5 to 8 inches high, the arching flower spike may reach 24 inches, with an abundance of flat, light lavender, 2-inch flowers, delicately spotted deep purple, which usually appear from autumn to early winter. Other selections in this genus have orange flowers with dark red spots.

Cycnoches
(SIK-noh-chees)
4" to 6"

The swan orchids resemble *Catasetum* and require the same culture. *Cycnoches warscewiczii* and *Cycnoches chlorochilon* are both lovely, with fragrant 5- to 7-inch yellow flowers. Any of the *Cycnoches* hybrids are recommended for under-lights culture.

Cymbidium
(sim-BID-ee-um)
8" to 3'

Popular for corsages, these terrestrial growers put forth spikes of waxy, long-lasting blooms. For the most flowers, select miniature oriental types or polymins, the hybrids between large cool-growing cymbidiums and small warm-growing species.

In temperate climates, set plants outside from June to October. They will accept full sun except during midday when they should receive high shade as that from tall trees. Indoors, place cymbidiums beneath four to six broad-spectrum

lamps that will have to be raised as spikes grow, because even the miniatures have 15- to 20-inch-long inflorescences. Choose some of the proven clones now available as mericlones. Standard cymbidiums are not only too large for growing in most light gardens, but usually also require cool 50 F autumn nights to set buds. The miniatures and polymins do well with 60 to 65 F nights.

Dendrobium
(den-DROH-bee-um)
4" to 6"

The dendrobiums differ so much in the requirements among species that it is necessary to consult orchid catalogs to select those suitable for your conditions. Among the most popular are the dwarf epiphytic *Dendrobium lindleyi* (syn. *Den. aggregatum*) with bright yellow flowers in spring and the spectacular *Dendrobium nobile* hybrids that grow to 2 feet. The *Dendrobium nobile* hybrids require 50 F nights in the autumn to bloom well. The Yamamoto hybrids are an excellent strain. All dendrobiums do best in small clay

Opposite left: Cymbidium Golden Elf 'Sundust' (ensifolium x Enid Haupt).
Opposite right: Color galore is available in dendrobiums — Dendrobium Kapalua 'Manabu' is among the many choices.
Top: Three-inch-tall Dendrobium cuthbertsonii, which is native to Papua New Guinea, comes in

several color forms. The pristine flowers last up to nine months each.
Above left: Dendrobium Super Star 'Dandy' (Malones x Utopia), a hybrid from Den. nobile.
Above: Dendrobium Yellow Chinsai 'Little Joe' (Chinsai x aureum) looks best when grown in a hanging container.

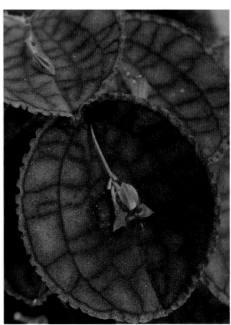

pots with reduced watering when not in active growth. Some of the smaller species grow well on cork-bark slabs.

Recent hybrids with *Dendrobium phalaenopsis*, sometimes combined with *Dendrobium canaliculatum*, offer compact growth with a multitude of 1- to 2-inch flowers. Hybridizers in Thailand and Hawaii have made some excellent compact dendrobium hybrids such as *Dendrobium* Muang Thai. A group of charming *Den. phalaenopsis compactum* hybrids that bloom when only 2 to 3 inches tall is now available. Read ads in current orchid periodicals and catalogs and visit commercial orchid growers to keep up to date on new hybrids.

Epidendrum
(ep-ee-DEN-drum)
4" to 8"

There are nearly 1,000 recognized *Epidendrum* species with several different growth habits. Best under lights are the compact epiphytes such as *Epidendrum anceps* with clusters of hay-scented green flowers, *Epidendrum ciliare* with

white 3- to 6-inch fringed flowers that appear several times per year, and the nearly everblooming *Encyclia* (syn. *Epidendrum*) *cochleata*, the cockleshell orchid, with yellow-and-dark-maroon flowers.

The semiterrestrial reed-stem epidendrums are easy to grow but must nearly touch the tubes to bloom satisfactorily. Crossing epidendrum species with cattleyas has created compact *Epicattleya* hybrids suitable for light gardens. Among the many choices are *Epc.* Frances Dyer (*C. bowringiana* x *Epi. fragrans*), with grape-colored flowers in the spring, and *Epc.* Epiorange (*Epi. alatum* x *C. aurantiaca*), which puts forth butter-yellow-colored flowers in the spring.

Laelia
(LAY-lee-ah)
2" to 4"

Laelias are epiphytes with flowers resembling small cattleyas. Numerous hybrids between *Laelia* and *Cattleya* have created an abundance of unusual showy orchids.

Pure species to grow under lights in-

clude *Laelia pumila*, a dwarf native to Brazil with round, sparkling, lavender flowers, and the white to lavender *Laelia rubescens* from Central America. Attach the plant to a slab of cork bark for best results. *Sophrolaelia* Psyche (*L. cinnabarina* x *Soph. coccinea*) is a 6-inch-tall red-orange-flowered hybrid that blooms several times a year when grown under lights.

Opposite left: Clusters of cheery flowers top the 12- to 18-inch-tall reedlike stems of *Epidendrum* (syn. *Oerstedella*) *capricornu*, a native of Peru.
Opposite right: Attractive foliage is a trademark of 3- to 4-inch-tall *Lepanthes tentaculata*.
Above left: Masdevallia Stella 'Greentree', AM-CCM/AOS (*coccinea* x *estradae*), grows 10 to 15 inches tall and flowers in the spring.
Above: Masdevallia datura bears fragrant flowers in the spring. It is the parent of several excellent hybrids, including *Masdevallia* Bella Donna, *Masdevallia* Night Stripes and *Masdevallia* White Swallow, which is warmth tolerant.

Lepanthes
(leh-PAN-theez)
6" to 8"

These epiphytes are true miniatures, $^1/_2$ to 1 inch tall with tiny jewellike yellow, green or maroon flowers on short spikes. Provide cool-to-intermediate (55 to 65 F) nights and high humidity. Species thrive when placed within an open-top terrarium under lights or in large glass Wardian cases. When grown in containers, use small clay types filled with unmilled sphagnum moss or tree-fern fiber that is kept evenly moist. Similar miniatures to grow with *Lepanthes* are *Masdevallia* and *Pleurothallis*.

Masdevallia
(mas-deh-VAHL-lee-ah)
3" to 12"

This genus includes miniatures and taller showy species, all from relatively cool mountain habitats in South America. Most of the cultivated species and hybrids mature at 6 to 8 inches tall, but a few such as *Masdevallia coccinea*, can reach 12 inches. Since masdevallias are compact they are ideal subjects for growing under lights. Fluorescent lamps are able to provide bright light without the damaging heat of the sun, which is perfect for cloud-forest genera. The recently introduced hybrids, including

many primary combinations between two species, are easier to grow than the pure species. Among the choices are the bright-orange *Masdevallia* Angel Frost (*veitchiana* x *strobelii*) and *Masdevallia* Redwing (*coccinea* x *infracta*), with red-toned flowers. Grow masdevallias in small pots filled with a mixture of fine bark and tree fern or rough New Zealand sphagnum moss.

Miltonia
(mil-TOH-nee-ah)
6" to 8"

Miltonias are epiphytes with sprays of flat flowers, sometimes called pansy orchids for the facelike markings. Species from lowland Brazil (*Miltonia clowesii*, *Miltonia spectabilis*) have 2- to 4-inch flowers that remain fresh when cut and placed in water.

The flowers of large-flowered, cool-growing species and their hybrids (*Miltonia vexillaria*, *Miltonia roezlii*) from higher altitudes last well only on the plant, in contrast to most other orchids that have a long cut-flower life.

These cooler-growing plants are sometimes sold as *Miltoniopsis*.

All of the miltonias, especially the vigorous hybrids, are suitable for light gardens. Look for *Miltonia* Goodale Moir (*flavescens* x *clowesii*), a yellow-flowered, warm-growing hybrid, and *Miltonia* Bremen (Limelight x Herrenhausen), a striking red-and-white, cool-growing hybrid. *Miltassia* is an excellent hybrid genus with *Brassia*, blooming on and off all year.

Neofinetia
(nee-oh-fih-NET-ee-ah)
4" to 8"

Neofinetia falcata, a 6- to 8-inch epiphyte, looks like a tiny *Vanda* with ridged succulent foliage forming small monopodial fans. Pristine white vanilla-scented flowers with long "tails" or "spurs" appear on 4- to 6-inch spikes.

Hybrids with a similar dwarf growth habit include *Ascofinetia* (x *Ascocentrum*) and *Nakamotoara* (x *Ascocentrum* x *Vanda*). Keep roots evenly moist because these plants lack pseudobulbs.

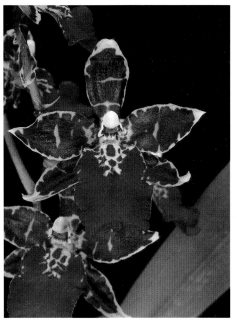

Odontoglossum
(oh-don-toh-GLOS-sum)
6" to 8"

Some *Odontoglossum* species from Mexico and Central America thrive with intermediate temperatures, but the classic *Odontoglossum crispum* hybrids, created from Andean species, must have cool 55 to 60 F nights. However, these epiphytes are all good choices for light gardens because they bloom well and grow easily in small pots of tree fern or unmilled sphagnum moss. Newer crosses combine other genera into artificial hybrids, usually more adaptable than straight species or plain cool-growing strains. Look for *Aspoglossum* (x *Aspasia*), *Colmanara* (x *Miltonia* x *Oncidium*) and *Odontocidium* (x *Oncidium*) to add to your collection.

Opposite left: Neofinetia falcata has been used to create compact-growing hybrids, including this *Neostylis* Lou Sneary (x *Rhynchostylis coelestis*). *Opposite right: Ascofinetia* Peaches 'Talisman Cove' (*Neof. falcata* x *Ascocentrum curvifolium*) is an ideal orchid for light gardens because it is compact and flowers two times a year. *Above: Odontoglossum* is in the background of

many *Oncidium*-like hybrids, including this *Colmanara* hybrid (*Colm.* Jungle Monarch 'Everglades' x *Lemboglossum bictoniense*). *Top:* Miniature-growing *Howeara* Mini-Primi (*Rodricidium* Primi x *Leochilus oncidioides*). *Above: Oncidium* Gower Ramsey (Goldiana x Guinea Gold) produces long-lasting sprays of dime-size flowers several times each year.

Oncidium
(on-SID-ee-um)
3" to 6"

The best-known oncidiums have sprays of 1- to 3-inch flowers with bright yellow lips. They are often called dancing-lady orchids. Grow these in small pots filled with bark or tree fern and provide air circulation. Try the compact species, such as *Oncidium ampliatum* (requires very strong light), *Oncidium cheirophorum* (a dwarf with fragrant yellow flowers from autumn to winter) and *Oncidium ornithorhynchum* (with sprays of fragrant rose flowers).

Oncidium Goldiana (*flexuosum* × *sphacelatum*) is a robust yet compact hybrid with sprays of golden flowers. *Oncidium* Gower Ramsey and *Oncidium* Sum Lai Wah grow well under broad-spectrum lights but may have to be moved into a sunny window once the 2- to 4-foot-long inflorescences begin to develop. Tolumnias (equitant oncidiums) are a suitable choice when grown close to wide-spectrum lamps or in an area fitted with high-intensity-discharge lamps.

Ornithocephalus
(or-nith-oh-SEFF-al-uss)
4" to 6"

These miniature epiphytes are best grown on slabs of tree fern. The common name mealybug orchid refers to the tightly packed spikes of fuzzy white flowers. Plants produce a flat fan of succulent foliage, interesting in itself. *Ornithocephalus bicornis* is 1 to 3 inches tall, while *Ornithocephalus grandiflorus* grows 4 to 6 inches. Look at the flowers under a magnifying glass.

Paphiopedilum
(paff-ee-oh-PED-ih-lum)
4" to 8"

The tropical slipper orchids grow as terrestrials on the jungle floor, on steep banks above streams or in mossy glens. They thrive under fluorescent lights and flowers last three to eight weeks on the plant. Some kinds have tessellated (marked with squares) foliage of deep green or silver, attractive all year. *Paphiopedilum* blooms are favored for black warts, erect stems, waxy pouches and glossy hairs.

Some slipper orchids have vertical stripes of white and green on the wide top sepal. Many species and their hybrids have black hairs all along the two side petals. The smooth plump pouch is a distinguishing feature of all paphiopedilums.

Intermediate to warm nights of 60 to 65 F are suitable for those species and hybrids with mottled foliage (*Paphiopedilum concolor*, *Paphiopedilum* Maudiae), while those paphiopedilums with plain green leaves make sturdier growth at 55 to 60 F.

Pot in a porous terrestrial medium. Suitable mixes are sold by commercial orchid growers or mix one by combining equal parts of medium to fine orchid bark, pasteurized houseplant potting-soil mix and coarse perlite. Keep roots evenly moist, but do not let pots sit in water.

Paphiopedilums need bright diffuse light, with relative humidity of at least 50 percent. The cool-growing slipper orchids, with plain green leaves, are more sensitive to low temperatures (50 to 55 F nights) for setting flower buds than to day-length. Studies with *Paphiopedilum*

Opposite left: Ornithocephalus inflexus will grow and flower when attached to a slab of tree fern. *Opposite right:* Many slipper orchids, including *Paphiopedilum* Red Magic (Gloriosum x fairrieanum), are ideal candidates for growing under lights. *Above:* Visiting orchid shows and nurseries will help you discover the excellent diversity to be found in *Paphiopedilum*, including this hybrid (wardii x philippinense var. roebelenii).

insigne show that this cool-growing species blooms well with short or long days if nights drop to at least 55 F. The same species exposed to 65 F night temperature did not set flower buds on long or short days. Such a temperature response (thermo-induction) of flower buds also occurs in standard cymbidium orchids that need cool nights to bloom.

Select the warmer-growing species and their hybrids unless you can drop the night temperatures to 55 F.

Hybrids are more adaptable than species so, although pure *Paph. insigne* may require cool 50 to 55 F nights to set buds, some of its hybrids bloom well when provided with warmer intermediate nights.

Paphiopedilum bellatulum is a dwarf-

Growing Orchids Under Lights

growing, warm-preference species from Thailand with creamy flowers lightly speckled maroon. Its short leaves are tessellated with dark green. Similar species for intermediate to warm nights are *Paphiopedilum concolor* and *Paphiopedilum niveum.*

All three are summer-blooming, but under lights they may have flowers at other seasons also.

Paphiopedilum glaucophyllum from Java has glaucous leaves, and produces dark-green and maroon flowers with hairy twisted petals on and off during the whole year.

Paphiopedilum sukhakulii is a variably colored species from Thailand but it always has lovely mottled foliage and flowers with a pointed yellow-and-rose-blushed pouch, white-to-yellow-toned petals with pubescent margins, and dark maroon dots.

Paphiopedilum venustum is a dwarf Himalayan species valued for the mottled foliage, deep purple underneath, and 2- to 3-inch waxy purple, green, and yellow flowers with a veined pouch.

Phalaenopsis
(fayl-eh-NOP-siss)
6" to 10"

Moth orchids, the common name for *Phalaenopsis*, are excellent for light gardens because the flowers last for weeks and plants are flat and low growing. They thrive with less light than many other showy orchids. Phalaenopsis are epiphytes, grow well in bark or tree-fern mixes, but must be kept lightly moist since they have no pseudobulbs. Satisfaction is guaranteed with any of them, especially the striking modern hybrids that bear flowers in white, yellow, pink or combinations with stripes or deep-colored lips.

Among compact species are *Phalaenopsis lueddemanniana* with fragrant, waxy, red-barred flowers, and *Phalaenopsis violacea* with 2- to 3-inch white flowers marked purple and green. Hybrids of these species tend to be more compact than standard white or pink selections.

When flowers fade, cut back the 1- to 3-foot-long inflorescence to just above a

lower node (a swollen area in the spike). This often prompts the plant to sprout a secondary inflorescence and thus doubles flower production. Hybrids with related genera are adaptable and often impart an exciting dimension to the orchid light garden. Look for these: *Asconopsis* (x *Ascocentrum*), *Doritaenopsis* (x *Doritis*) and *Renanthopsis* (x *Renanthera*).

Pleurothallis
(plur-oh-THAL-liss)
4" to 8"

These are generally dwarf 2- to 6-inch-tall plant forming tufts of foliage with small sprays of tiny flowers, best appreciated under a magnifying glass. Charming cool to intermediate epiphytes for limited space, pleurothallis often thrive mounted on slabs of tree fern or in 1- or 2-inch thumb pots. *Pleurothallis*

Opposite left: Renanthopsis Fiery Gem (*Renanthera* Brookie Chandler x *Phalaenopsis* Zada) combines the bright red of renanthera with the compact habit of phalaenopsis.
Opposite right: A Phalaenopsis hybrid (Sambambo x *lueddemanniana*).
Top: Many phalaenopsis hybrids are available today, including *Phalaenopsis* Miami Golden Anniversary (Gypsy x *stuartiana*).
Above: Phalaenopsis are among the orchids with peloric flowers that are becoming increasingly popular. *Phalaenopsis* Mama Cass 'Talisman Cove' (Ida Fukumura x Cassandra) has three-lipped flowers.

truncata is a small plant bearing $^1/_8$-inch brilliant orange flowers along lax inflorescences. Only 2 inches tall, *Pleurothallis tribuloides* bears brick-red, beak-shaped flowers. *Pleurothallis schiedei*, 3 inches tall, has brown-marked sepals with peculiar waxy appendages dangling from them.

Polystachya
(pol-ee-STAK-ee-ah)
4" to 8"

This is one of the few genera to be found in both the Old and New World Tropics. Species are epiphytes that thrive in small pots of tree fern or unmilled sphagnum. *Polystachya luteola* has 8- to 10-inch erect spikes of fragrant, yellow-green flowers on compact 8- to 12-inch-tall plants. Dwarf-growing *Polystachya fallax* bears fragrant white flowers with yellow and red markings.

Rodriguezia
(rod-reh-GEEZ-ee-ah)
4" to 9"

These intermediate- to warm-growing epiphytes thrive on slabs of tree fern or in small pots of tree fern. The plants seldom grow above 6 inches, but arching flower spikes may reach 10 inches.

Rodriguezia granadensis from Colombia has 2-inch white flowers with yellow in the lip. *Rodriguezia venusta* is similar. *Rodriguezia lanceolata* (syn. *secunda*) bears 1-inch bright rose flowers several times during the year.

Hybrids with *Oncidium*, called *Rodricidium*, are dwarf and free-flowering, making them excellent candidates for growing under lights.

Sarcochilus
(sar-koh-KYE-luss)
4" to 6"

The Australian orange blossom orchid, *Sarcochilus falcatus*, has short spikes of fragrant white flowers dotted red. It flowers from winter to spring. The compact plants, which can be grown on pieces of tree fern or cork or in a small container, should be cultivated under humid, warm conditions.

Sophronitis
(sof-roh-NYE-tiss)
6" to 8"

Orange and red flowers have made these dwarf Brazilian epiphytes famous as parents in orchid hybrids. *Sophronitis* is bred with the much larger cattleyas, laelias, brassavolas and related genera to impart dark orange to flame tones and dwarf growth to hybrids. Straight species are not necessarily easy to grow, but with high humidity and when attached to bark slabs or logs, they can be grown under lights. Fall-to-winter-blooming *Sophronitis cernua* (1-inch orange-red flowers) and *Sophronitis coccinea* (syn. *grandiflora*) with vermilion 1- to 3-inch flowers are available from species specialists. Hybrids using *Sophronitis* as one parent, such as *Slc.* Bellicent (*Soph. coccinea* x *Laeliocattleya* Bonanza), are compact and more adaptable than pure *Sophronitis*.

Opposite left: One- to 2-inch-tall *Pleurothallis grobyi* bears 6-inch-tall inflorescences.
Top left: Grow *Stanhopea tigrina* in a slat basket so the pendent inflorescences can emerge easily.
Top right: Sophronitis has been bred with other members of the *Cattleya* Alliance to create small-growing plants. *Sophrolaeliocattleya* Katie's Jewel

'Talisman Cove' (*Sc.* Carol Lynn x *Slc.* Tangerine Jewel) has 2¹/₄-inch flowers on a 6-inch-tall plant. This plant was grown and flowered under broad-spectrum fluorescent lamps.
Above: Compact-growing *Sophrolaelia* Jinn 'Yellow Sparkler', JC/AOS (*Laelia milleri* x *Soph. coccinea*) flowers winter into spring.

Stanhopea
(stan-HOHP-ee-ah)
6" to 8"

Above: Long-lasting flowers are borne on this compact-growing *Vanda* hybrid (Keeree's Blue x *coerulea*), which was 8 inches tall when it flowered for the first time.

Stanhopeas grow wide, dark green leaves up to 12 inches long and form round pseudobulbs. Large 3- to 5-inch fragrant waxy flowers in white, yellow or cream with maroon dots open on a spike that grows directly down from the pseudobulbs. Pot in an open-slat basket with tree fern, sphagnum moss or osmunda fiber; suspend the basket under the lamps.

Although stanhopeas are too large for many light gardens, they are easy to grow and require only moderate light to bloom well. *Stanhopea oculata* (vanilla- or chocolate-scented, 4- to 5-inch red-purple flowers in summer) and *Stanhopea eburnea* (fragrant 5- to 6-inch white flowers in autumn) are spectacular, although their flowers last only five to eight days.

Stelis
(STEE-liss)
6" to 8"

This genus contains almost 500 species, mostly ½- to 4-inch epiphytes with sprays of small cream-to-yellow flowers. Some *Stelis* species grow on moss-covered rocks and on twigs in the cloud forests of South America. In captivity, they need high humidity, cool-to-intermediate nights and a potting medium through which water passes quickly. Pot in unmilled sphagnum moss, or mount on slabs of tree fern. They are at home in a collection of similarly dwarf *Pleurothallis, Masdevallia* and *Lepanthes*.

Vanda
(VAN-dah)
2" to 12"

Vandas hybridized with *Ascocentrum*, called *Ascocenda*, are better suited to light gardens than pure vandas, which grow too tall. Many ascocendas have flowers resembling vandas, but the plants are smaller (10 to 24 inches tall). *Ascocenda* hybrids come in all vanda colors and patterns.

Foliage Orchids for Under Lights

SEVERAL terrestrial orchids are treasured for their jewellike foliage. They do well under medium light, even with cool white-warm white combinations. A terrarium is also excellent for these low-growing jewel orchids. All are tropical except *Goodyera pubescens*, a native of eastern North America. Pot these small terrestrials in humus-rich soil. Keep roots evenly moist but never soggy and provide 60 to 70 percent humidity.

Anoectochilus
(ah-nek-toh-KYE-luss)
12" to 24"
   Anoectochilus roxburghii and *Anoectochilus sikkimensis* are similar creepers with bronze-green foliage netted gold. When trailing stems get bare, cut a 3- to 4-inch growing tip section to root in moist sphagnum moss.

Goodyera
(good-YER-ah)
12" to 24"
   The pointed and pliable leaves of

Above: Anoectochilus roxburghii, prized for its attractive foliage, thrives when grown in its own container or in a dish garden with small ferns.

Goodyera pubescens, rattlesnake plantain, are variegated white and green. It makes a compact specimen in a terrarium or a container. *Goodyera pubescens* is a cold-hardy native and long a favorite for New England partridge-berry terrariums. Provide diffused light and temperatures of 50 to 70 F. It provides several years of beauty in a terrarium landscape maintained under fluorescent tubes.

Ludisia
(loo-DISS-ee-ah)
10" to 20"
   This plant, known for years as *Haemaria discolor*, is a robust Malayan species with dark purple-green leaves netted red or gold. Specimens may reach 8 inches with the white flowers appearing on short spikes from the velvety new growth.

12 ~ Sources for Supplies

EQUIPMENT FOR GROWING ORCHIDS under lights is easy to obtain from various mail-order sources. Some basic equipment, such as standard fluorescent fixtures and timers, will be found at local hardware stores. More-specialized items, such as light-garden carts, trays, wall-mounted fixtures and agricultural high-intensity-discharge lamps, are listed in the catalogs mentioned below.

Check recent orchid-society periodicals, such as *Orchids — The Magazine of the American Orchid Society*, for advertisements offering light-garden equipment and supplies.

To locate plants for a light garden, consult orchid magazines and the *Orchid Source Directory*, which is issued every two years and given to every member of the American Orchid Society. It includes a listing of growers and suppliers who sell orchid plants suitable for growing under lights. Orchid plants can also be found at orchid nurseries and orchid shows.

Berkeley Indoor Garden Center
844 University Avenue
Berkeley, California 94710
Tel 510-549-2918
E-mail info@berkelyindoorgarden.com
Web site www.berkleyindoorgarden.com
High-pressure sodium, low-pressure sodium, metal halide and full-spectrum fluorescent lighting.

Charley's Greenhouse Supply
17979 State Route 536
Mt. Vernon, Washington 98273
Tel 800-322-4707; 360-428-2626
E-mail customerservice@charleysgreenhouse.com
Web site www.charleysgreenhouse.com
Orchid grow lights, digital light meter, other supplies for growing orchids under lights. Catalog available.

Full Spectrum Lighting
27 Clover Lane
Burlington, Vermont 05401
Tel 800-261-3101; 802-863-3100
Lamps (Wonderlite® and Swivelier®), stands, fixtures, timers and trays, and other supplies. Free catalog.

Gardener's Supply Company
128 Intervale Road
Burlington, Vermont 05401
Tel 800-688-5510; 800-863-1700
E-mail info@gardeners.com
Web site www.gardeners.com
Some supplies for indoor gardening. Free catalog.

Hydrofarm Gardening Products
3135 Kerner Boulevard
San Rafael, California 94901
Tel 707-765-9990; 707-765-9977
Web site www.gardenindoors.com
High-intensity-discharge (HID) halide and sodium lamps. Free catalog. Branch offices: 4720 Indianola Avenue, Columbus, Ohio 43214 (telephone 800-833-6868, 614-885-4600; e-mail columbus@gardenindoor.com) and 208 Route 13, Bristol, Pennsylvania 19007 (telephone 800-227-4567, 215-781-0304; e-mail philadelphia@gardenindoors.com).

Indoor Gardening Supplies
PO Box 527AO
Dexter, Michigan 48240
Tel 800-823-5740; 866-823-4978
E-mail igs@indoorgardensupplies.com
Web site www.indoorgardensupplies.com
Light-garden carts, lamps, trays, timers, capillary matting, meters, books and accessories for light gardening. Free catalog.

OFE International, Inc.
PO Box 161302
Miami, Florida 33116

Tel 305-253-7080; 305-251-8245
E-mail sales@OFE-INTL.com
Web site www.OFE-INTL.com
Potting mixes, fertilizers, books and other products suitable for the under-lights grower. Catalog US$3.

Orchids by Hausermann
2N 134 Addison Road
Villa Park, Illinois 60181-1191
Tel 630-543-6855; 630-543-9842
E-mail info@orchidsbyhausermann.com
Web site www.orchidsbyhausermann.com
Orchid Garden light stand, trays and lamps. Free catalog.

Sunlight Supply®, Inc.
5408 Northeast 88th Street, #A-101
Vancouver, Washington 98665
Tel 888-478-6544; 360-883-8846
Fax 360-883-5395
E-mail info@sunlightsupply.com
Web site www.sunlightsupply.com
Supplementary lighting systems, custom ballasts, reflectors, replacement lamps and components, light meters and timers. Free catalog.

Above: One way to obtain new orchids is by ordering them through the mail. Reliable nurseries guarantee safe arrival, in part because they pack the plants securely, like the orchids shown here. Advertisers sell plants through orchid journals, including *Orchids — The Magazine of the American Orchid Society.*

Venture Lighting International, Inc.
32000 Aurora Road
Solon, Ohio 44139
Tel 800-338-6161; 440-248-0600
E-mail venture@adlt.com
Web site www.venturelighting.com
This manufacturer specializes in metal-halide-lamp technology. Informative free folders explain the open-fixture Energy Master™ metal-halide lamps.

Verilux
9 Viaduct Road
Stamford, Connecticut 06907
Tel 800-786-6850; 203-921-2430
E-mail info@verilux.net
Web site www.verilux.net
Manufacturers of Instant Sun full-spectrum fluorescent lamps, known for true-color rendering. Free illustrated folder.

13 ~ Recommended Reading

THESE RESOURCES ARE USEFUL TO gardeners interested in more detail about growing orchids under lights.

American Orchid Society

The American Orchid Society is a 501(c)(3) nonprofit organization founded in 1921 to extend the knowledge, production, use and appreciation of orchids. Today, this 30,000-member Society is the preeminent orchid-related organization in the world. Members receive a monthly award-winning magazine (*Orchids*), a free copy of *Your First Orchid* (when they join), the *AOS Orchid Source Directory*, a 10 percent discount in The AOS BookShop and Orchid Emporium, free admission to the International Orchid Center in Delray Beach, Florida, answers to their questions and more. For information on the International Orchid Center, AOS membership or to request a free brochure: American Orchid Society, 16700 AOS Lane, Delray Beach, Florida 33446 (telephone 561-404-2000; fax 561-404-2100 e-mail TheAOS@aos.org; Web site orchidweb.org).

Periodicals

Australian Orchid Review This bimonthly magazine is filled with articles on the cultural needs of orchids. A section devoted to cymbidiums is in each issue. Available from Australian Orchid Review, 14 McGill Street, Lewisham, New South Wales, 2049 Australia.

Orchid Digest A quarterly publication issued by the Orchid Digest Corporation. *Orchid Digest* offers a balance of cultural articles and essays focusing on the taxonomy and scientific study of orchids. Available from Orchid Digest, PO Box 1216, Redlands, California 92373-0402 (Web site www.orchiddigest.org).

The Orchid Review The Royal Horticultural Society prints this colorful maga-

zine six times a year. Articles discuss specific groups of orchids as well as orchids in nature and their cultural needs. Available from Orchid Review, RHS Subscription Service, PO Box 38, Ashford, Kent, TN25 6PR, United Kingdom (e-mail orchidreview@rhs.org; Web site www.rhs.org.uk/about/mn_pubs_journals_orchid.asp).

Orchids Australia This is the official publication of the Australian Orchid Council. Issued every two months (February, April, June, August, October, December), this magazine emphasizes the cultural needs of orchids. Available from Orchids Australia, PO Box 145, Findon, South Australia 5023 (e-mail orchids@cgnet.com.au; Web site www.infoweb.com.au/orchids/).

Orchids — The Magazine of the American Orchid Society This monthly, award-winning magazine offers a useful balance between basic culture information and advanced growing techniques. An extensive advertising section offers supplies and orchid plants. A yearly index makes finding specific features an easy task. Information on *Orchids* is available from the American Orchid Society.

Orchid Books

The following books are published by the American Orchid Society:

Growing Orchids. 2002 Revised Edition. Written by experts, this book explains how to grow popular orchid genera and discusses cultural techniques.

Orchid Pests and Diseases. 2002 Revised Edition. Practical advice on raising healthy orchids with new information on biological controls and a glossary.

Your First Orchid, by Stephen R. Batchelor. 2001 Revised Edition. Basic introduction to growing orchids with step-by-step information.

For a single book that offers botanical

details and brief culture notes on most of the cultivated genera, see *The Manual of Cultivated Orchid Species* by Helmut Bechtel, Phillip Cribb and Edmund Launert. Other books of value to anyone growing orchids under lights are *All About Growing Orchids* by Rick Bond (Ortho Books, San Ramon, 1998), *Home Orchid Growing* by Rebecca Tyson Northen (Van Nostrand Reinhold Co., New York. 4th edition, 1990), *Taylor's Guide to Orchids* by judywhite (Houghton Mifflin Co., Boston. 1996), *Orchids* by Greg Allikas and Ned Nash (Thunder Bay Press, San Diego. 2000), *Orchids* by Elvin McDonald (Sunset Books, Melno Park. 1998), and *You Can Grow Orchids,* by Mary Noble McQuerry (published by author. 5th revised edition, 1987). These are available from The AOS BookShop, which issues a booklist containing more than 150 orchid-related titles plus videos, CDs and other educational materials. The booklist can be viewed on line at the Society's Web site (orchidweb.org) or a free copy is available from The AOS BookShop, 16700 AOS Lane, Delray Beach, Florida 33446 (telephone 561-404-2020; fax 404-2100; e-mail TheAOS@aos.org).

American Orchid Society offers dozens of colorful photographs, including this cover image of *Galeandra greenwoodiana* 'Orchid Art', CHM/AOS.

Catalogs

GE Lighting Lamp Catalog This thick, illustrated catalog shows precise data for all GE lamps, including fluorescents, tungsten and high-intensity discharge. Consult this publication if you plan on building an extensive light gardening range. Request from General Electric Company, Nela Park, Cleveland, Ohio 44112 (telephone 216-266-2121). An e-catalog is also available for downloading from GE's Web site (www.gelighting.com).

Philips Lighting Lamp Specification and Application Guide This 124-page guide offers suggestions on choosing specific Philips lamps for various applications. Philips also offers folders covering horticultural lighting. Available from Philips Lighting Company, Somerset, New Jersey 08875 (telephone 1-800-555-0050; Web site www.lighting.philips.com).

Internet Orchid Resources

Several sites on the Internet are devoted to orchids and the number of sites is growing constantly. Prime among these is *OrchidWeb®* (http://orchidweb.org). Maintained by the American Orchid Society, this site offers advice for growing orchids in the greenhouse, in the home and under lights, and explains how to deal with pests and diseases that affect orchids. There is also a calendar of orchid events and an orchid-judging schedule.

Other sites:

Canadian Orchid Congress (www.canadianorchidcongress.ca/)

The Orchid House (http://retirees. uwaterloo.ca/~jerry/orchids/)

Orchid Mall (www.orchidmall.com)

Orchid Safari (http://anam.keltik.net/ nuchat/)

Index

Entries indexed include major subject headings and binomials in *italics*. Page numbers in **boldface** indicate illustrations.

Growing Orchids Under Lights

Growing Orchids Under Lights

International Orchid Center

THE American Orchid Society's International Orchid Center is a popular destination for anyone wishing to see live, flowering orchids and learn more about this dynamic family of flowering plants.

Conveniently located between Interstate 95 and the Florida Turnpike in Delray Beach, Florida, it offers:

• Educational presentations and programs.

• More than three-and-a-half acres of beautiful theme gardens, including a rainforest, Florida native habitat, formal garden, and the Lewis and Varina Vaughn Garden, which was built in loving memory of the Society's greatest benefactors.

• An orchid-filled greenhouse where visitors may stroll and enjoy the flowers.

• Seasonal displays of flowering orchids in a specially designed trellis.

• The Orchid Emporium, a tantalizing gift shop offering books, clothing, accessories and more.

Future additions for the orchid campus include a two-story library and an 80-seat auditorium for ongoing orchid education. AOS members are admitted to the International Orchid Center free of charge. Please come by for a visit — and then come again to enjoy new flowering orchids and witness botanical wonders as they unfold in our subtropical garden.

INTERNATIONAL ORCHID CENTER
16700 AOS Lane
Delray Beach, Florida 33446-4351
Tel 561-404-2000 • Fax 561-404-2100
E-mail TheAOS@aos.org
Web site orchidweb.org
The AOS BookShop and Orchid Emporium
Toll free 1-877-ORCHIDS or 561-404-2020

American Orchid Society
Founded In 1921

Acknowledgments

Thanks to the following for their assistance in providing technical details related to specific lamps mentioned in this book: Brandy Bolt, horticulturist, Hydrofarm, San Rafael, California; Richard A. Crossen, Manager of Product Planning, Venture Lighting International, Solon, Ohio; Nicholas G. Harmon, President, Verilux Co., Stamford, Connecticut; and Indoor Gardening Supplies staff, Detroit, Michigan. Hydrofarm Gardening Products gave permission to print the illustrations on pages 33 and 39.

Special appreciation is given to authors Kenneth M. Rossman and S. Robert Weltz Jr, who shared their experiences with growing orchids under HID lamps.

I am grateful to the following American Orchid Society staff members who helped prepare this book: Arlene Maguire, Jane Mengel, Ned Nash, Sylvia Wood, Susan Jones and James Watson.